Sweet
MONSTA,
Pin-Up's

COLORING BOOK

BY CHRISTINA GIBBS

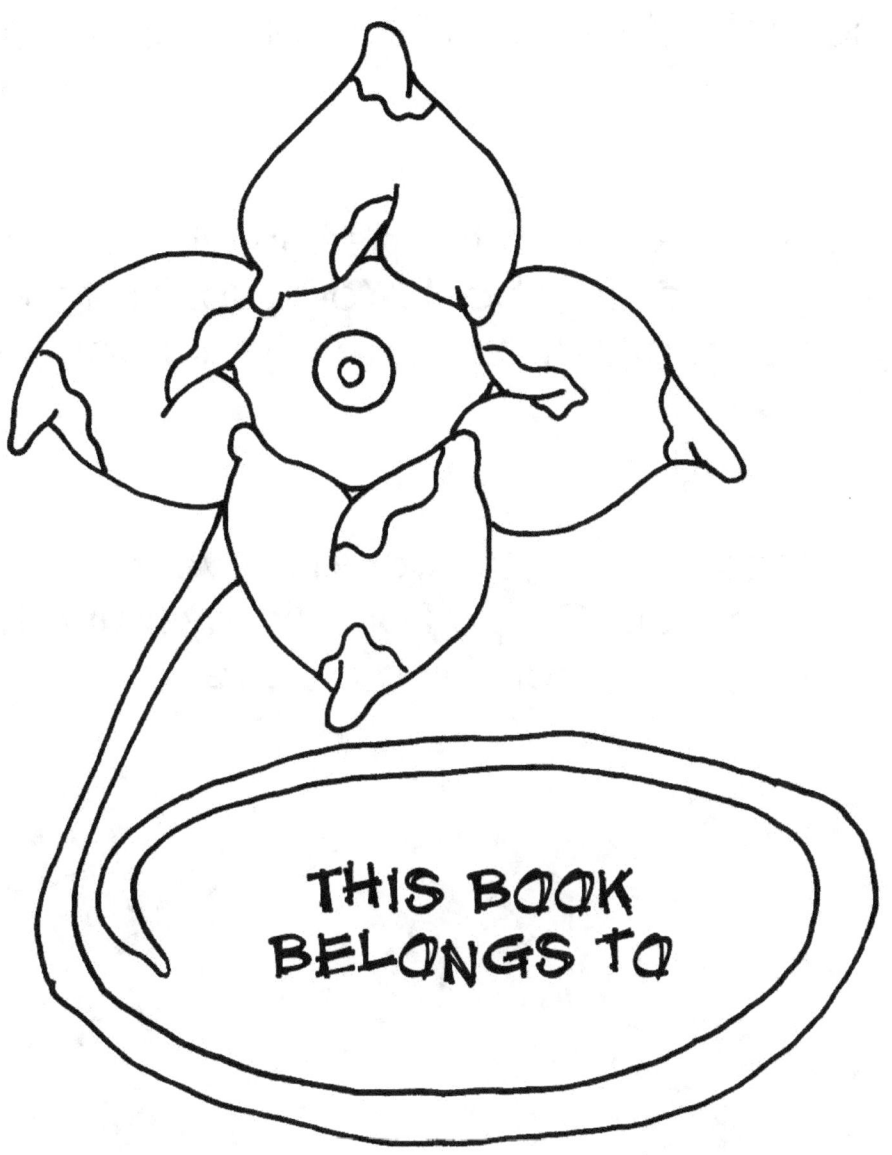

THIS BOOK
BELONGS TO

_____

_____

This book is dedicated to my family and friends who motivated me to keep drawing. I love you.

Huge thank you to the person who purchased my first coloring book. Your support towards my art is greatly appreciated. Thank you so much.

Dad, I know you would be very proud of me. Your Chrissy Pooh finally found her drawing groove.

"Pooh, Don't EVER give up"
-Daddy

Through these pages you will find beautiful
pin-up's with delicious cupcakes to match them.
I love desserts as much as I love to draw. With
that being said, I wanted to add a touch of sweetness
to my monstas.

I chose cupcakes because you can transform them
into anything you want with just a little imagination.
Just like you can with monsters. I didn't want a typical
"ugly" monster. I wanted to give mines a more girly feel to
them.

I hope you enjoy coloring in my beauties. It was such a
joy to create them for you. I'm very pleased on how they
came out. I hope you are as well.

GRAB YOUR PENCIL

GET COMFORTABLE

LETS COLOR!

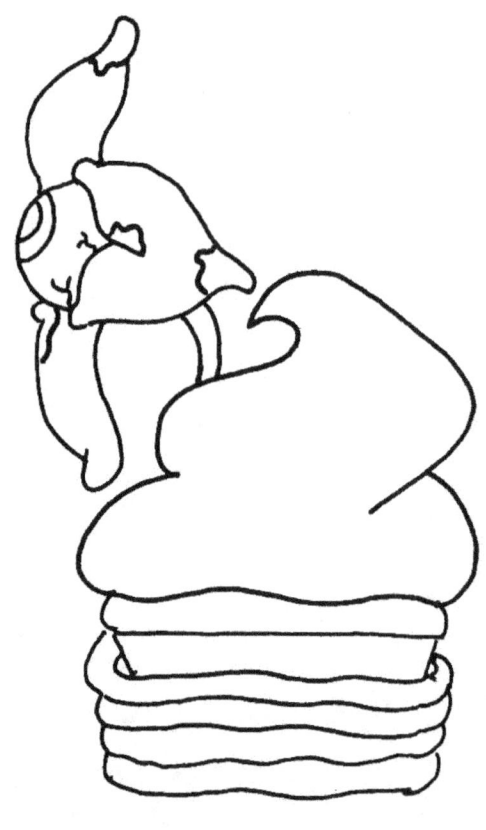

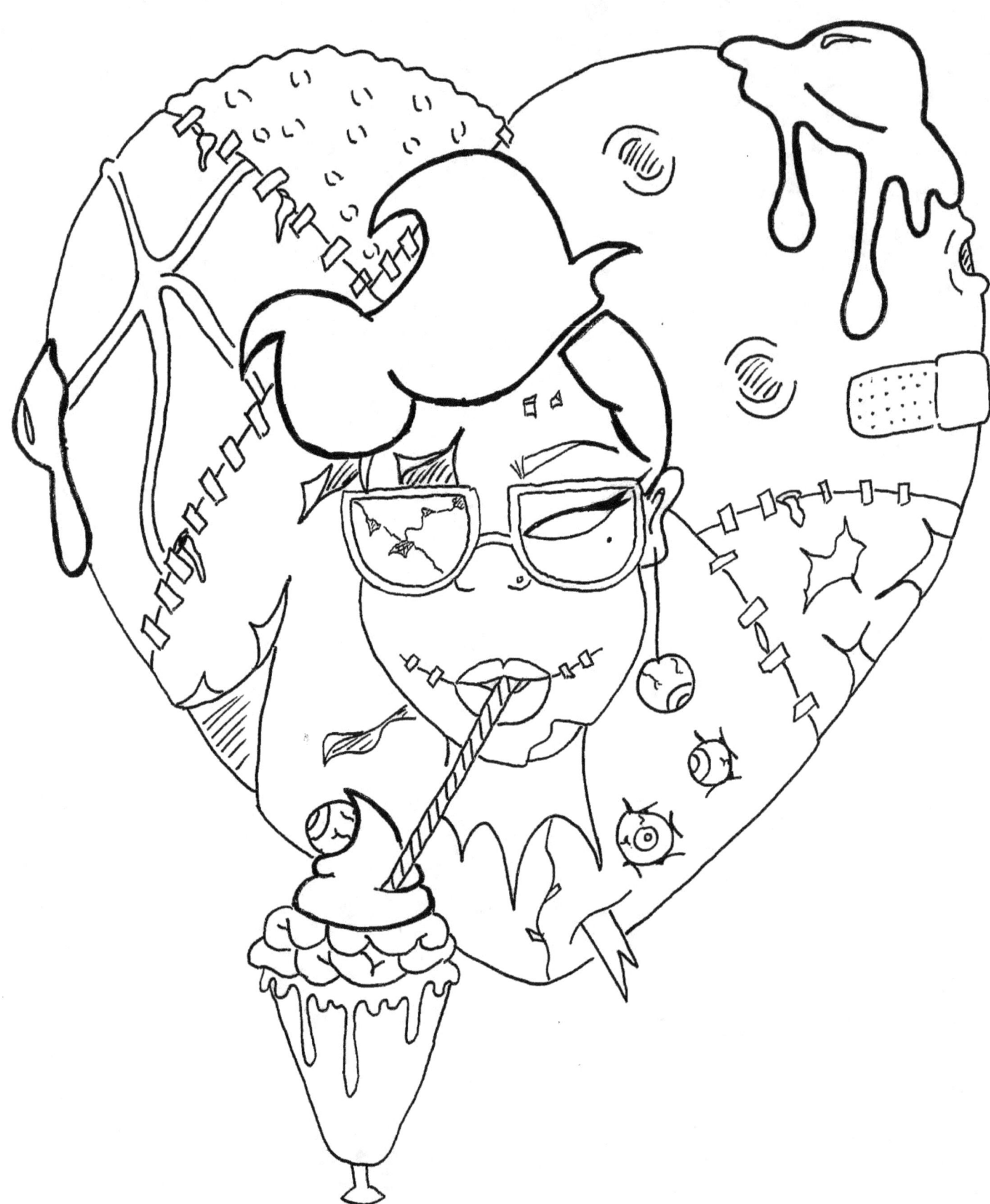

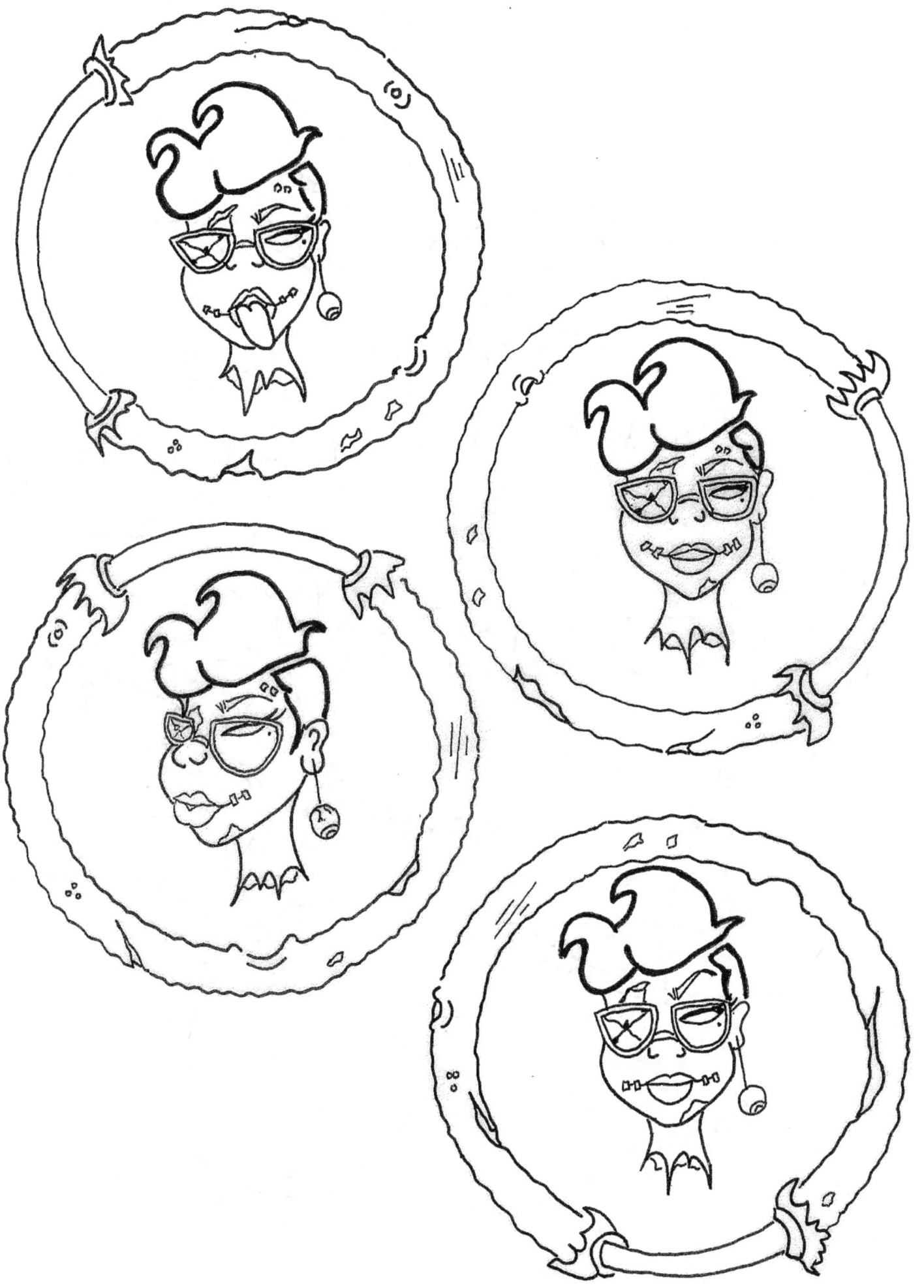

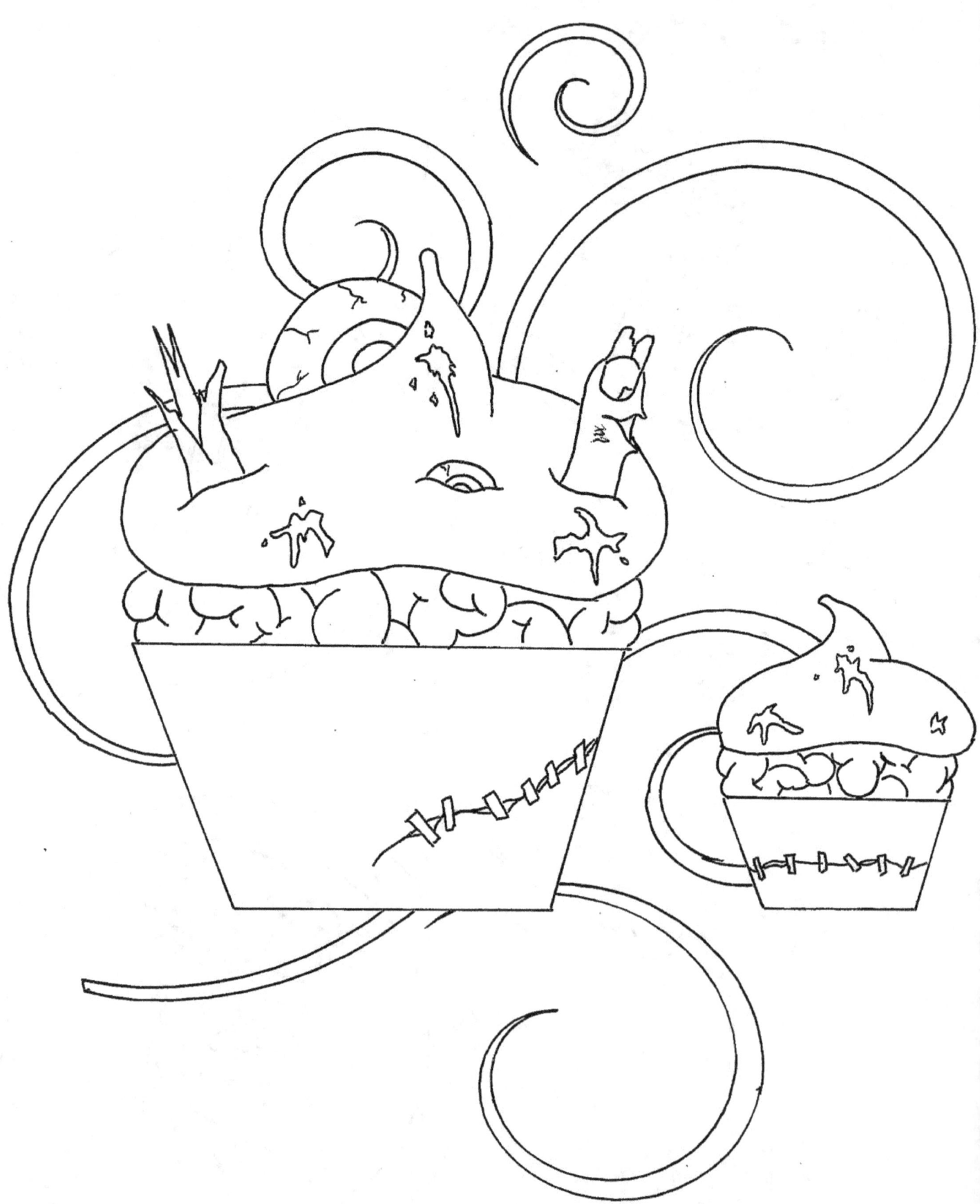

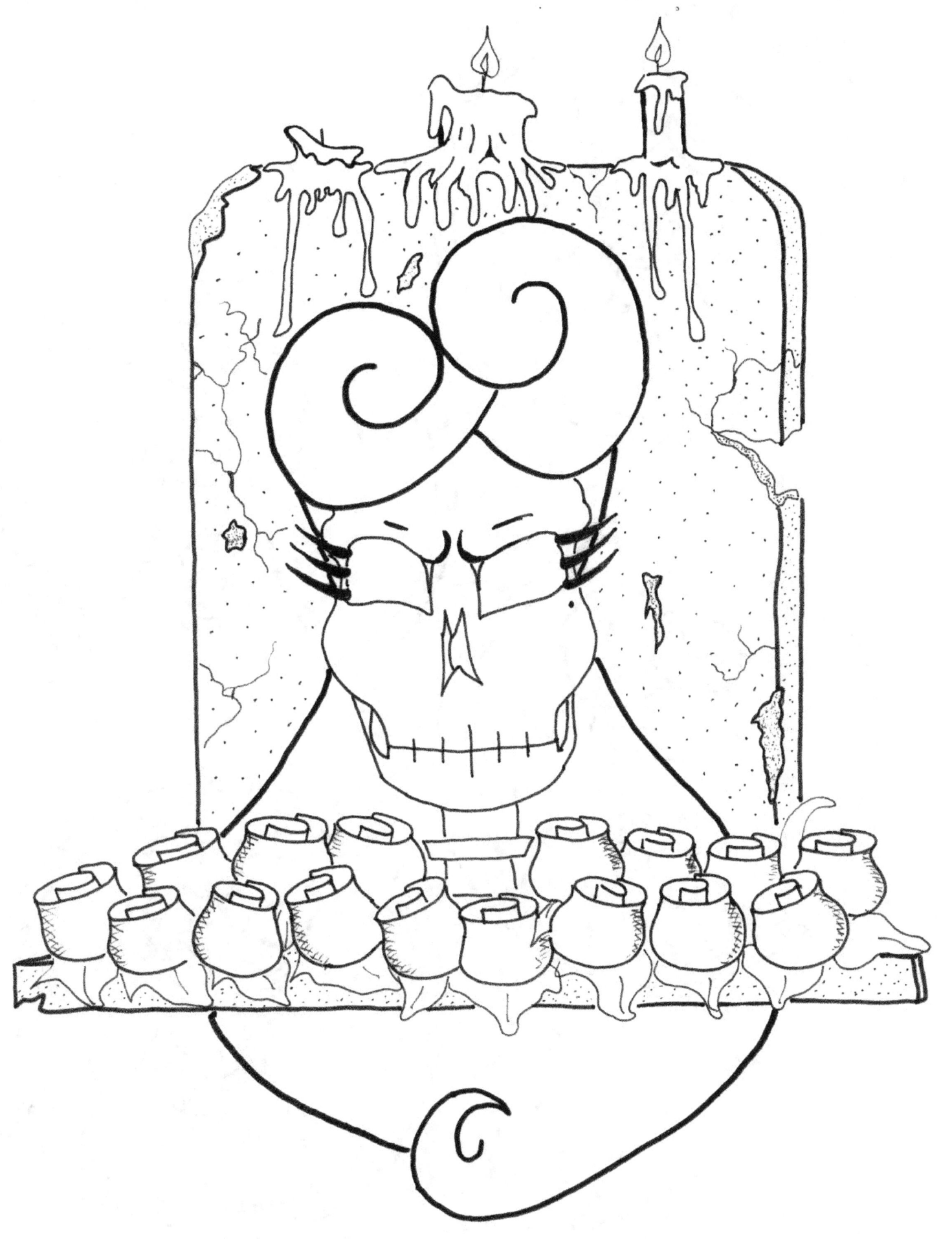

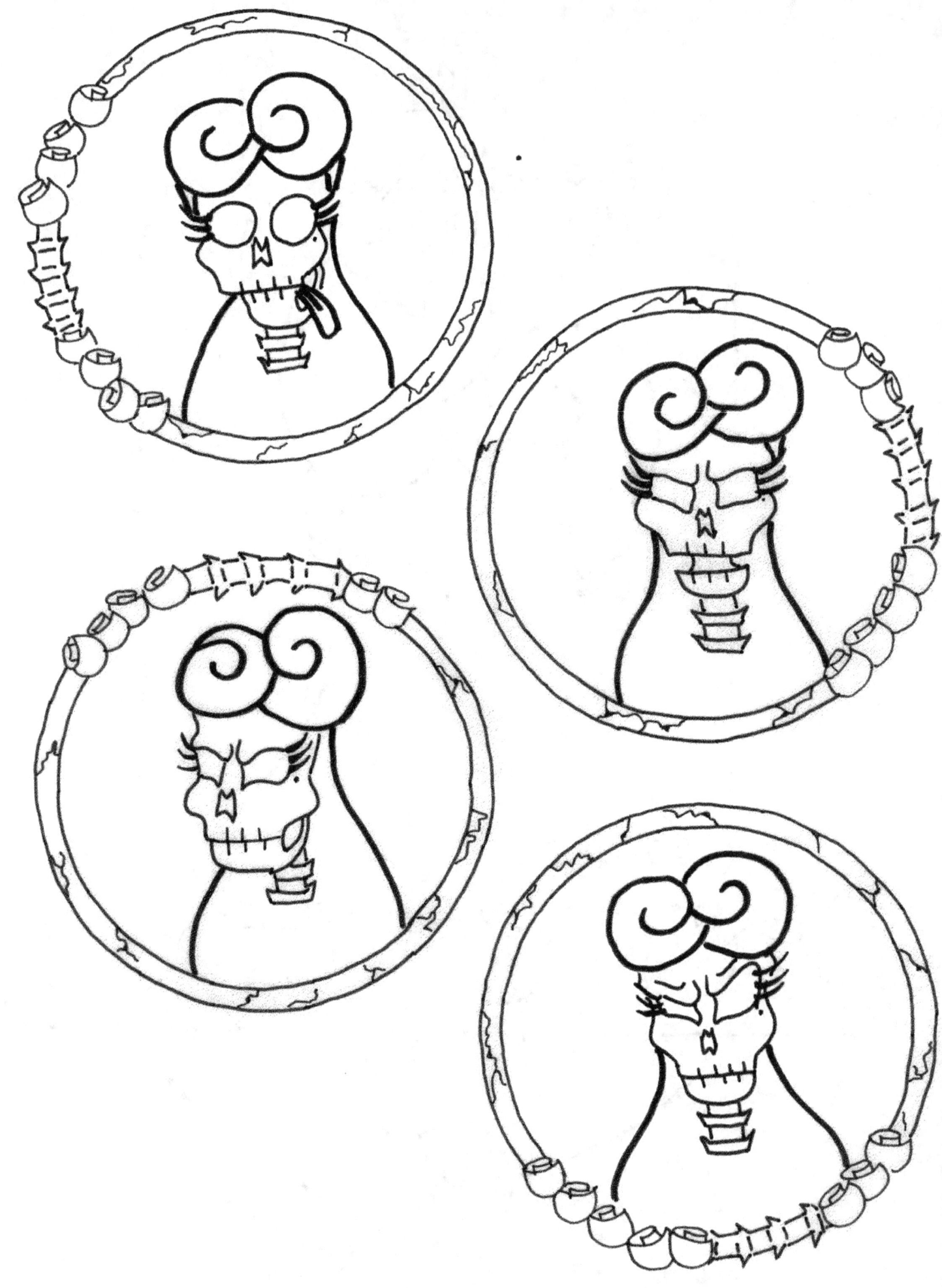

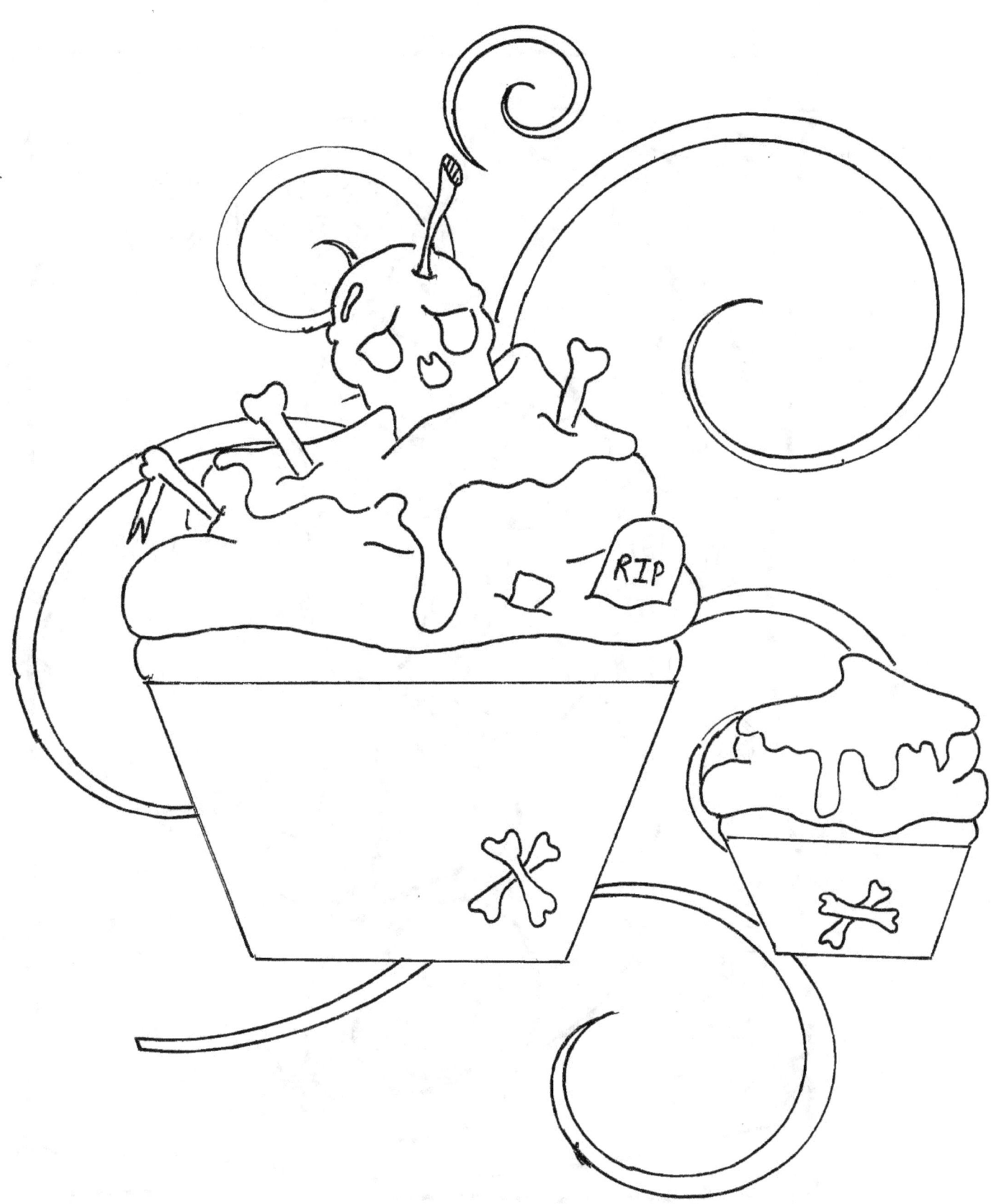

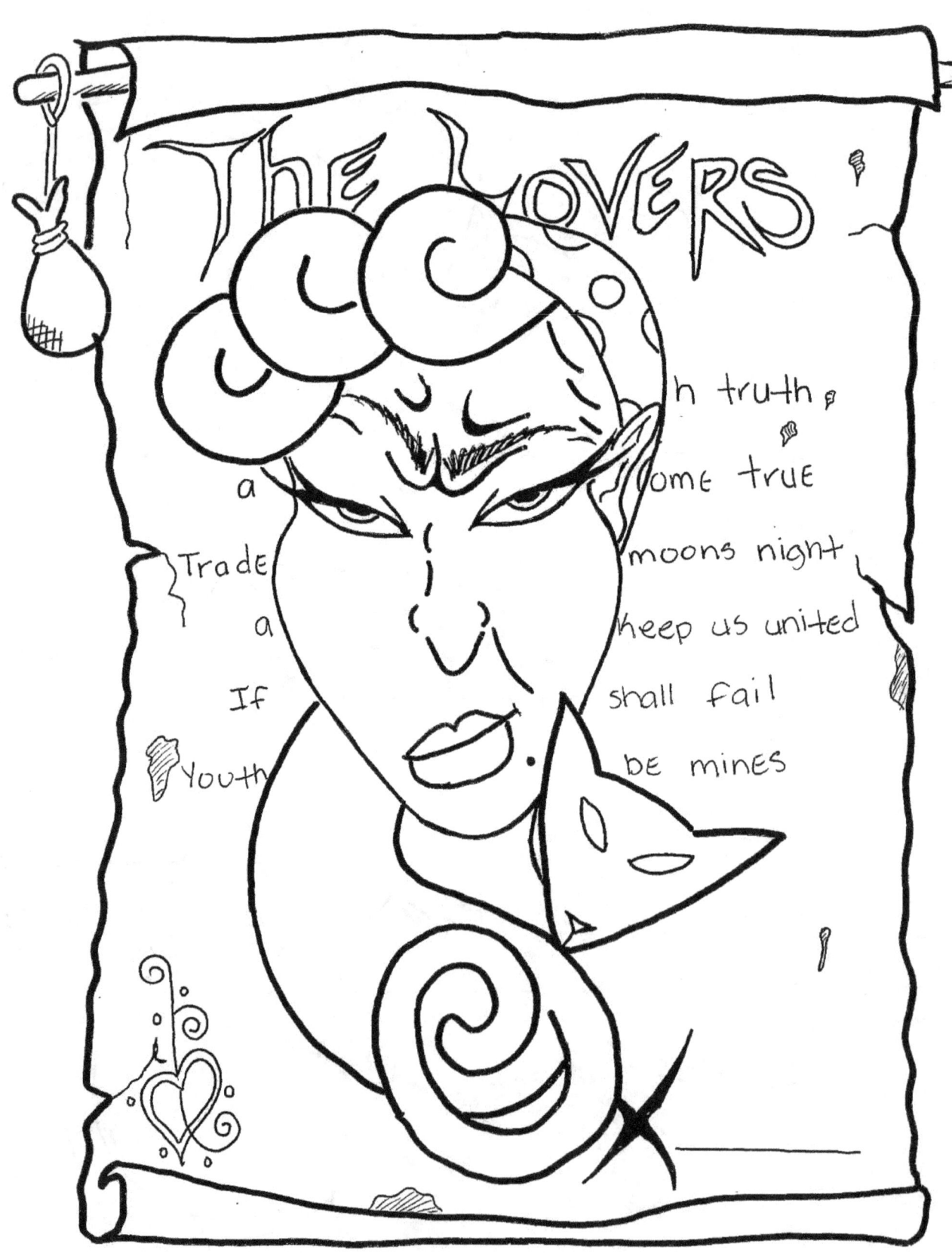

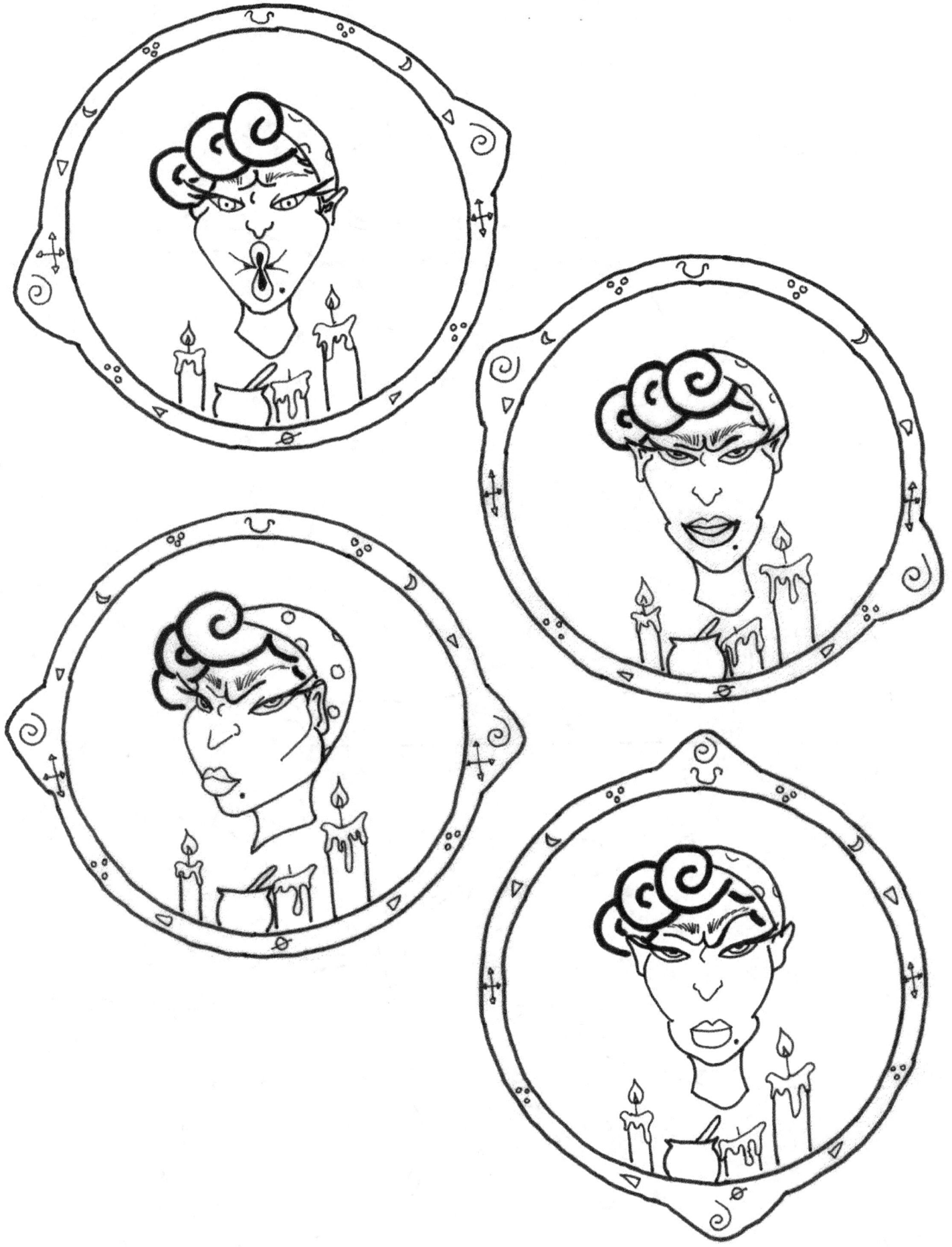

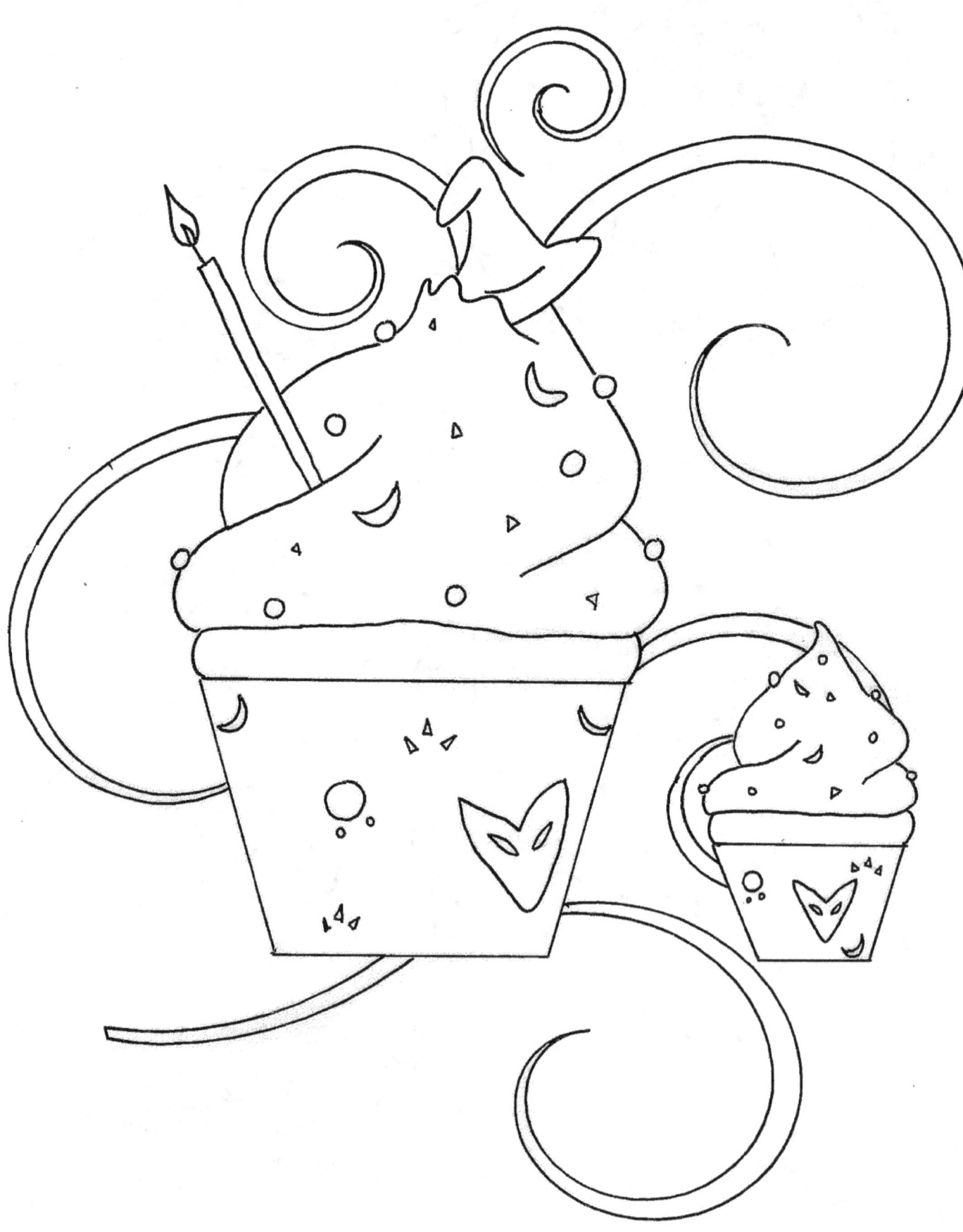

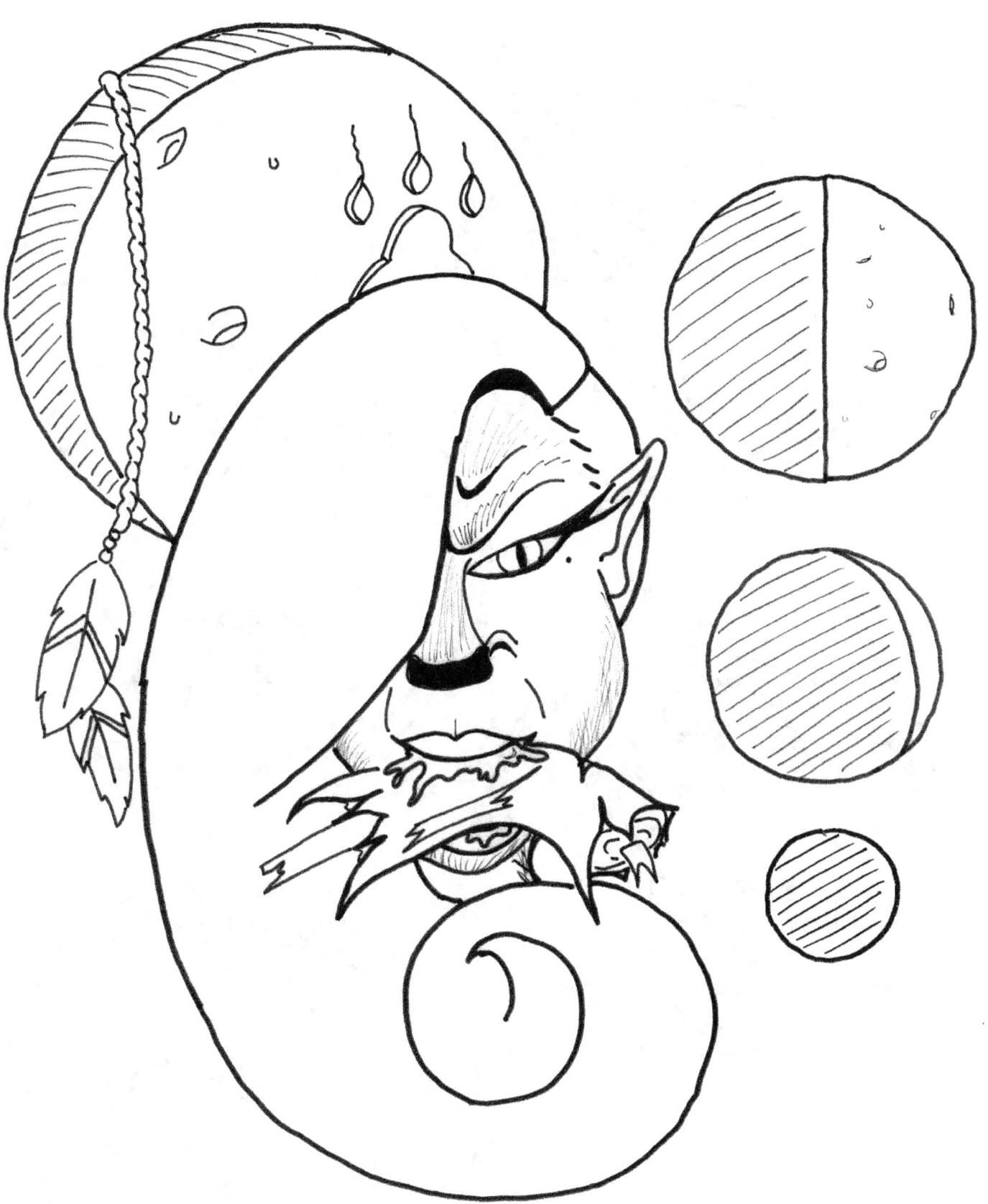

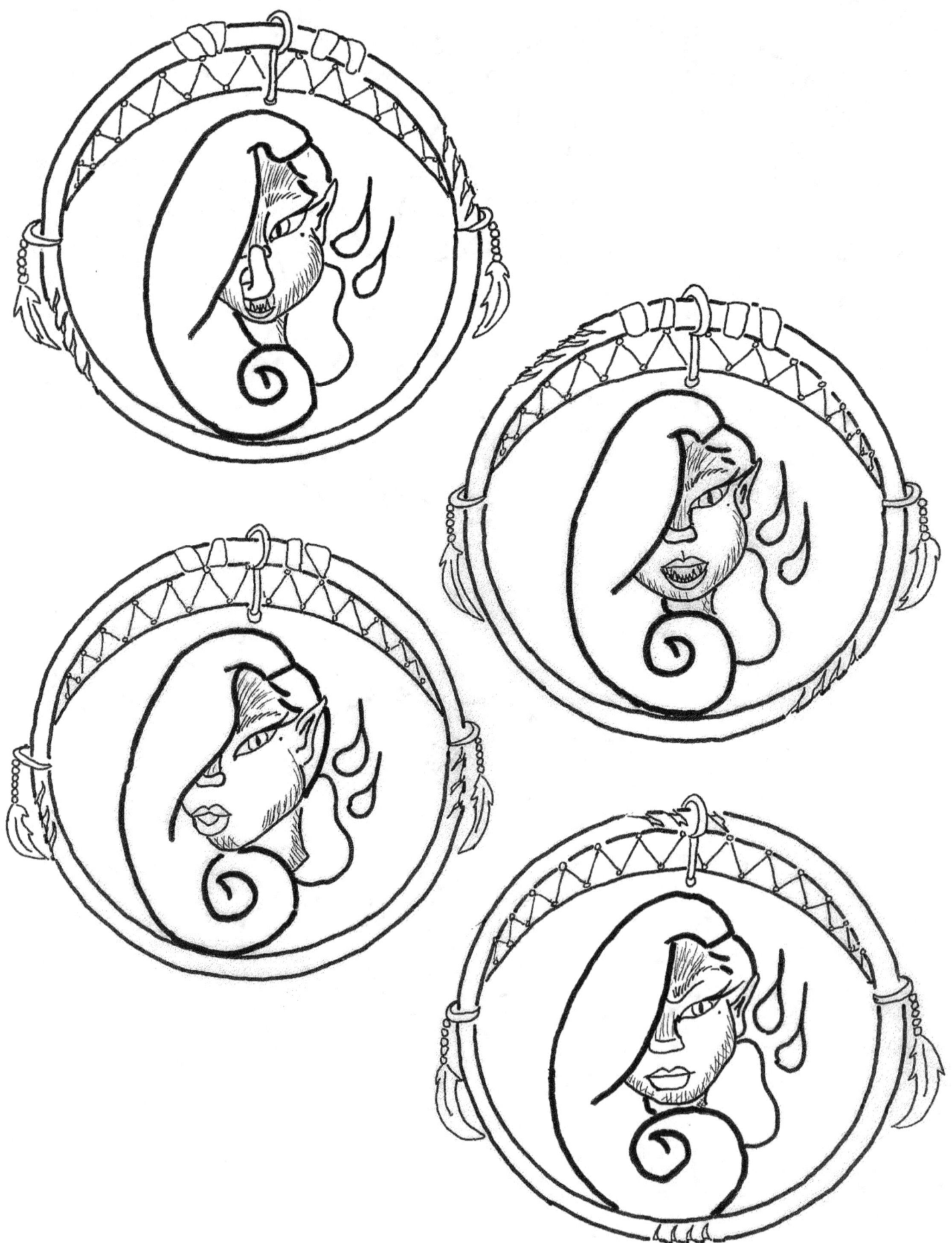

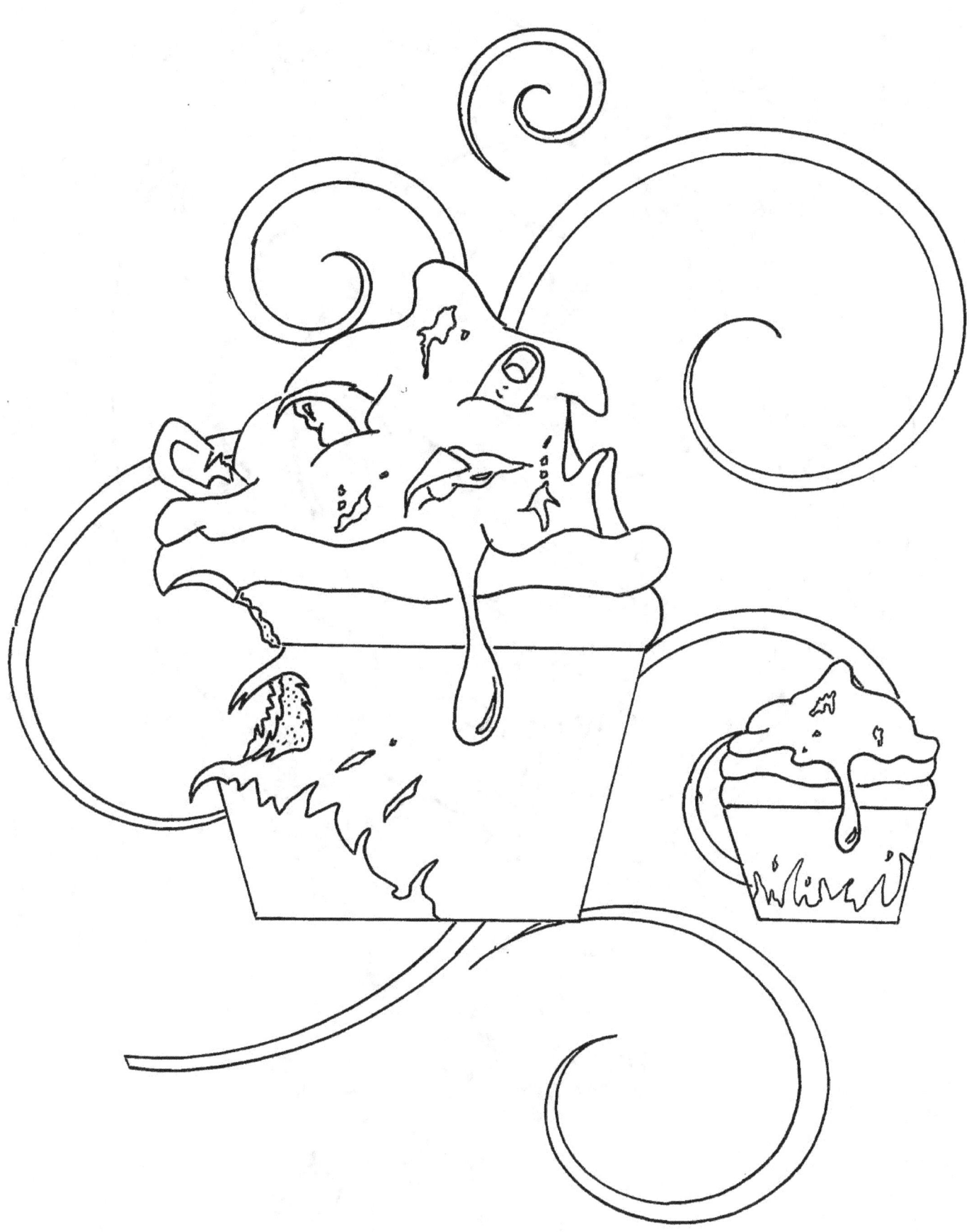

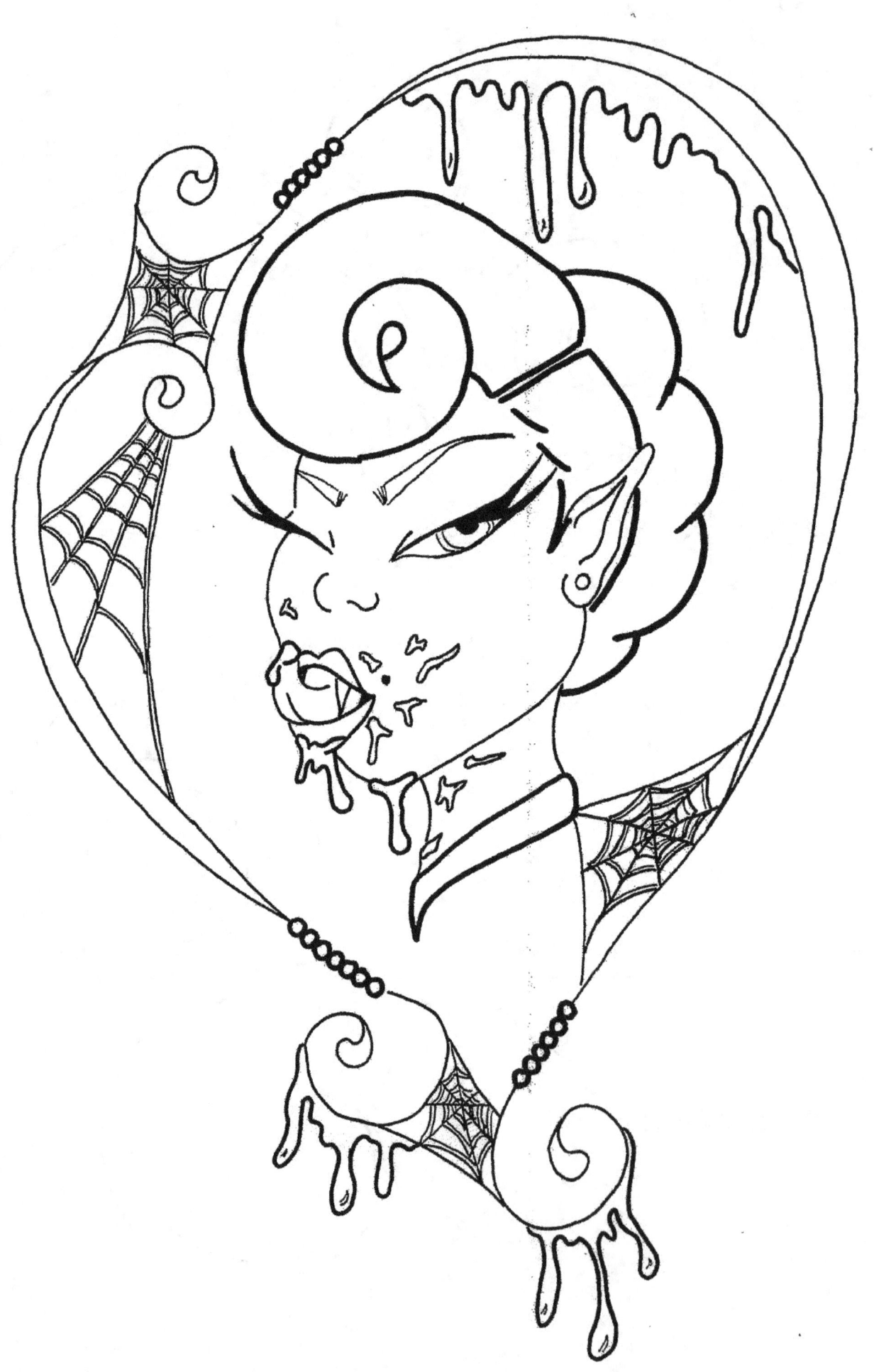

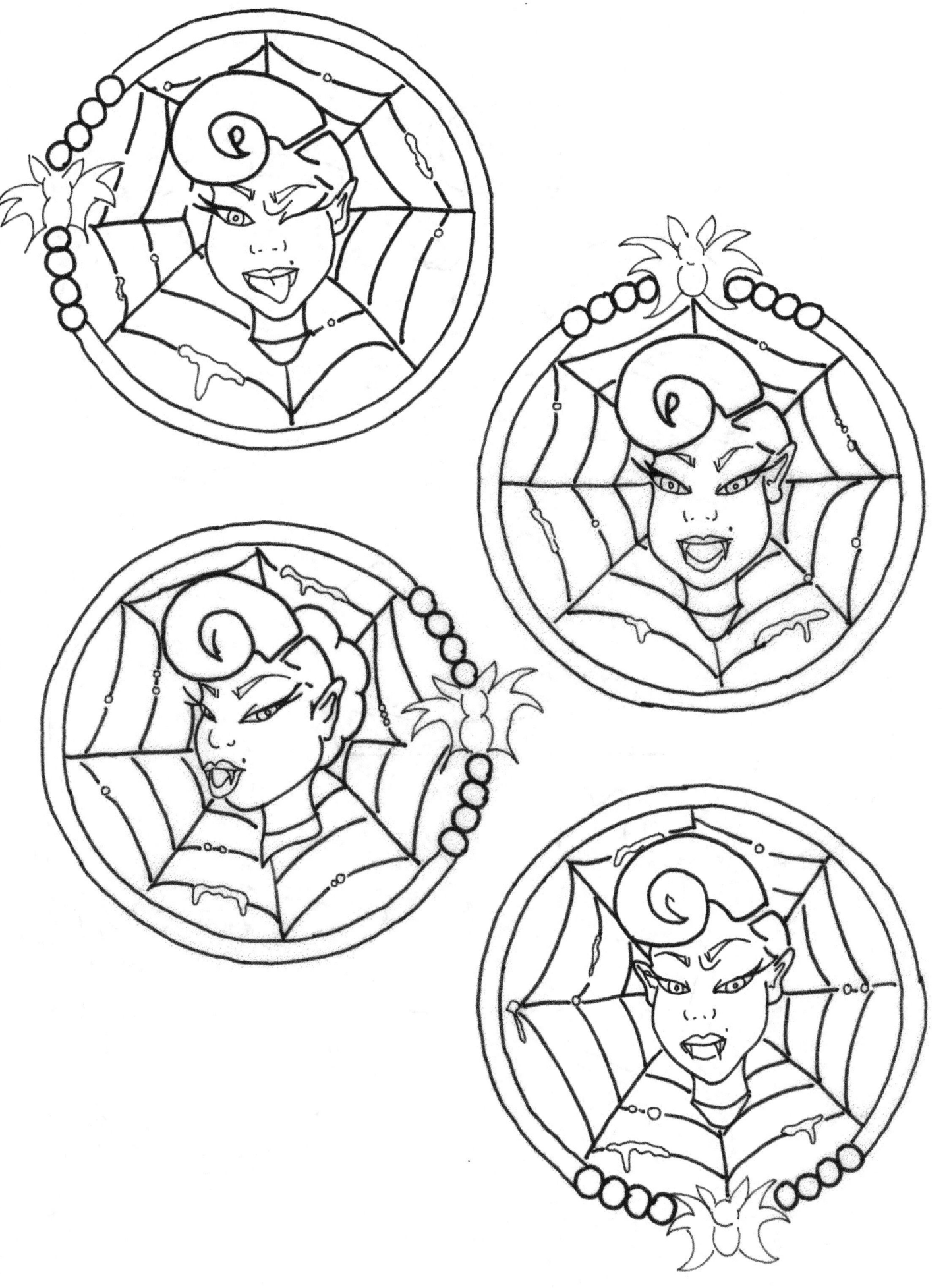

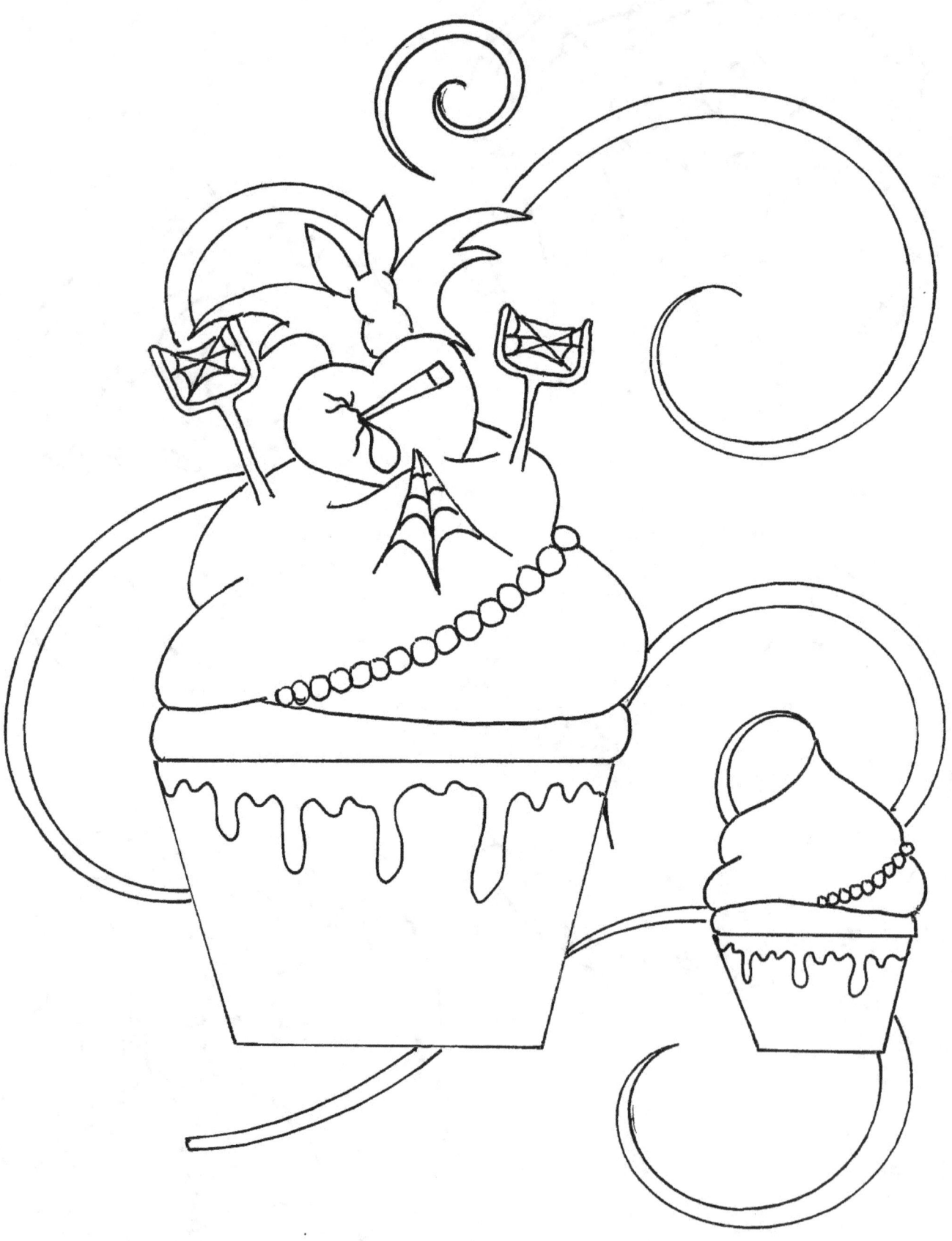

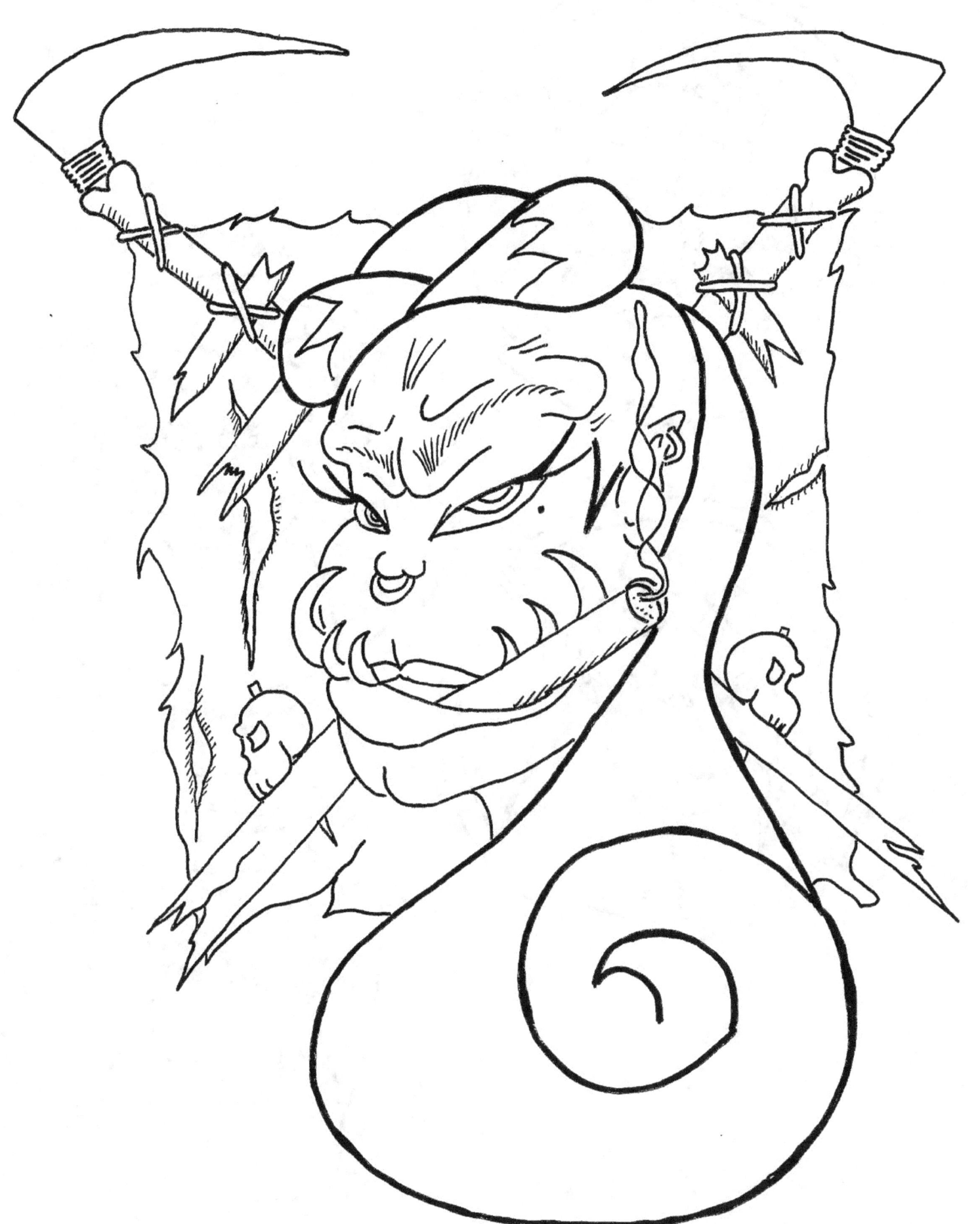

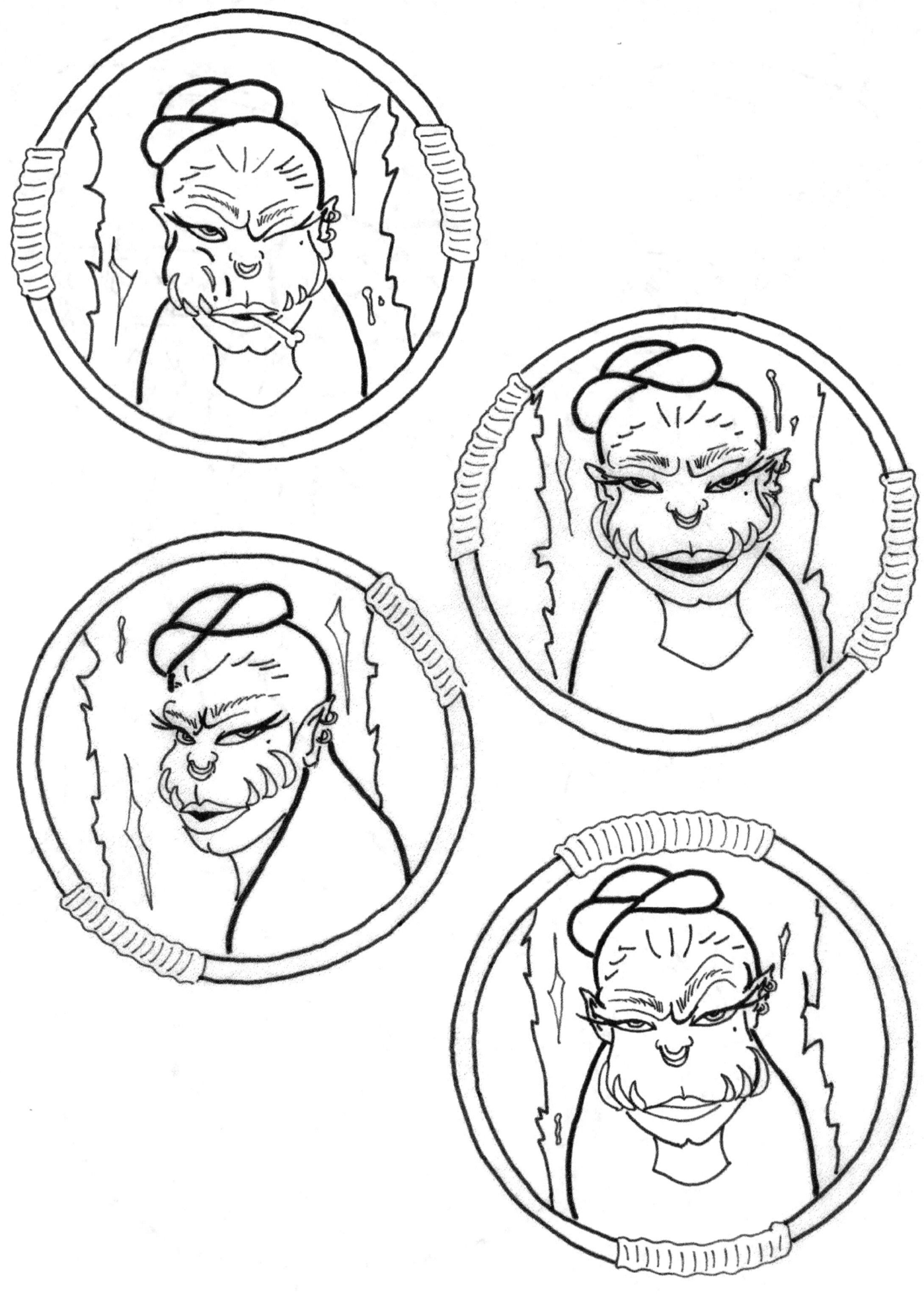

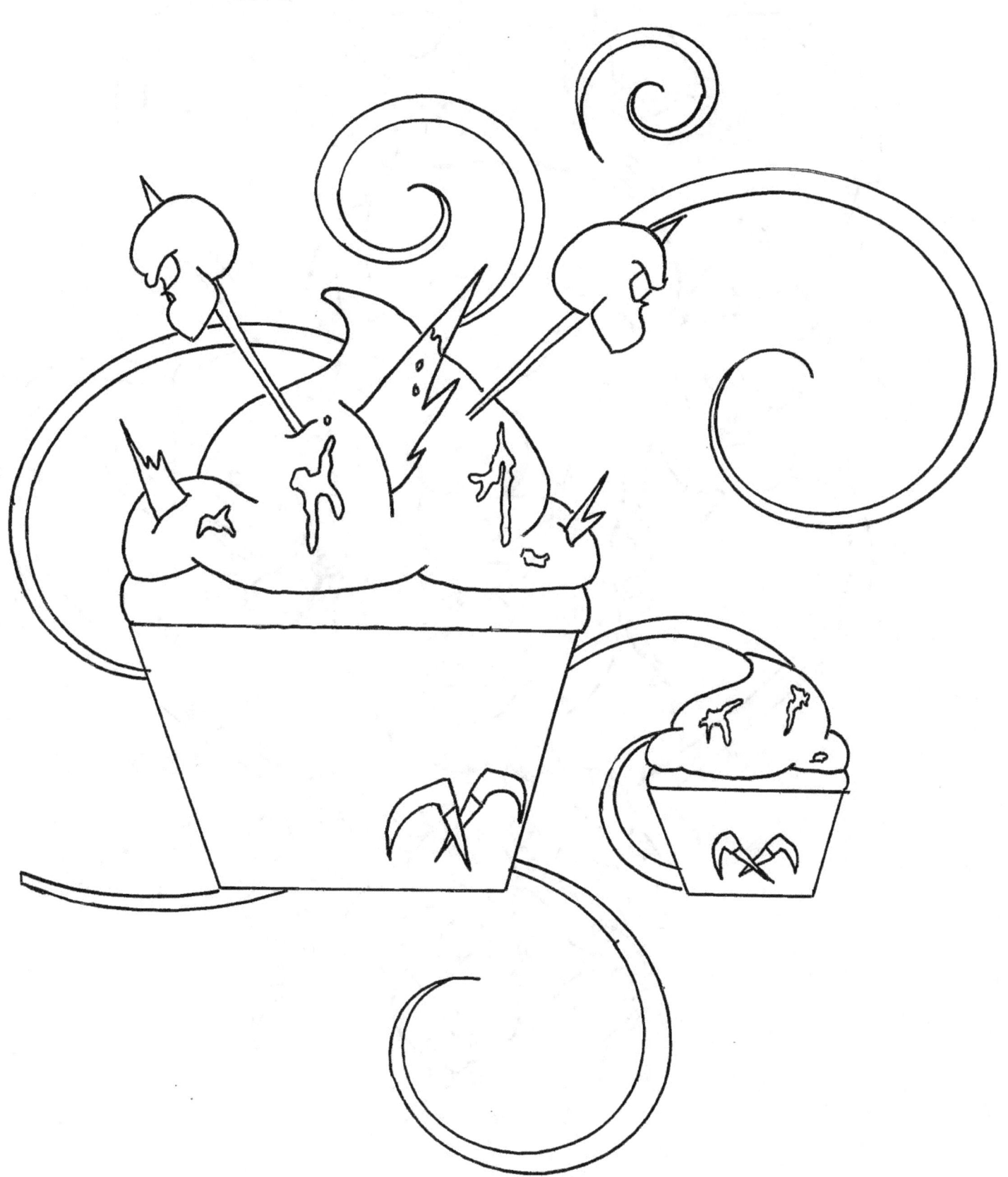

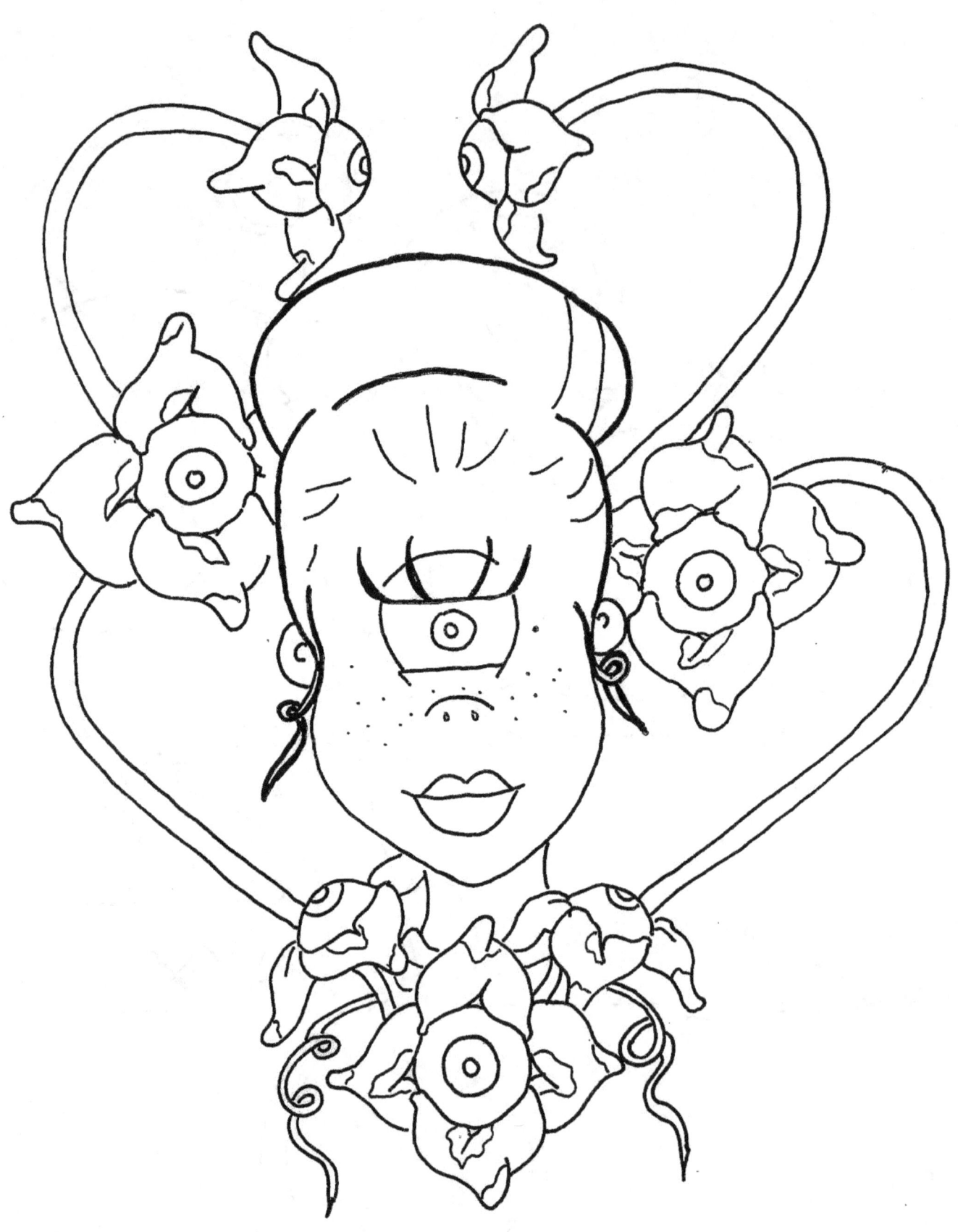

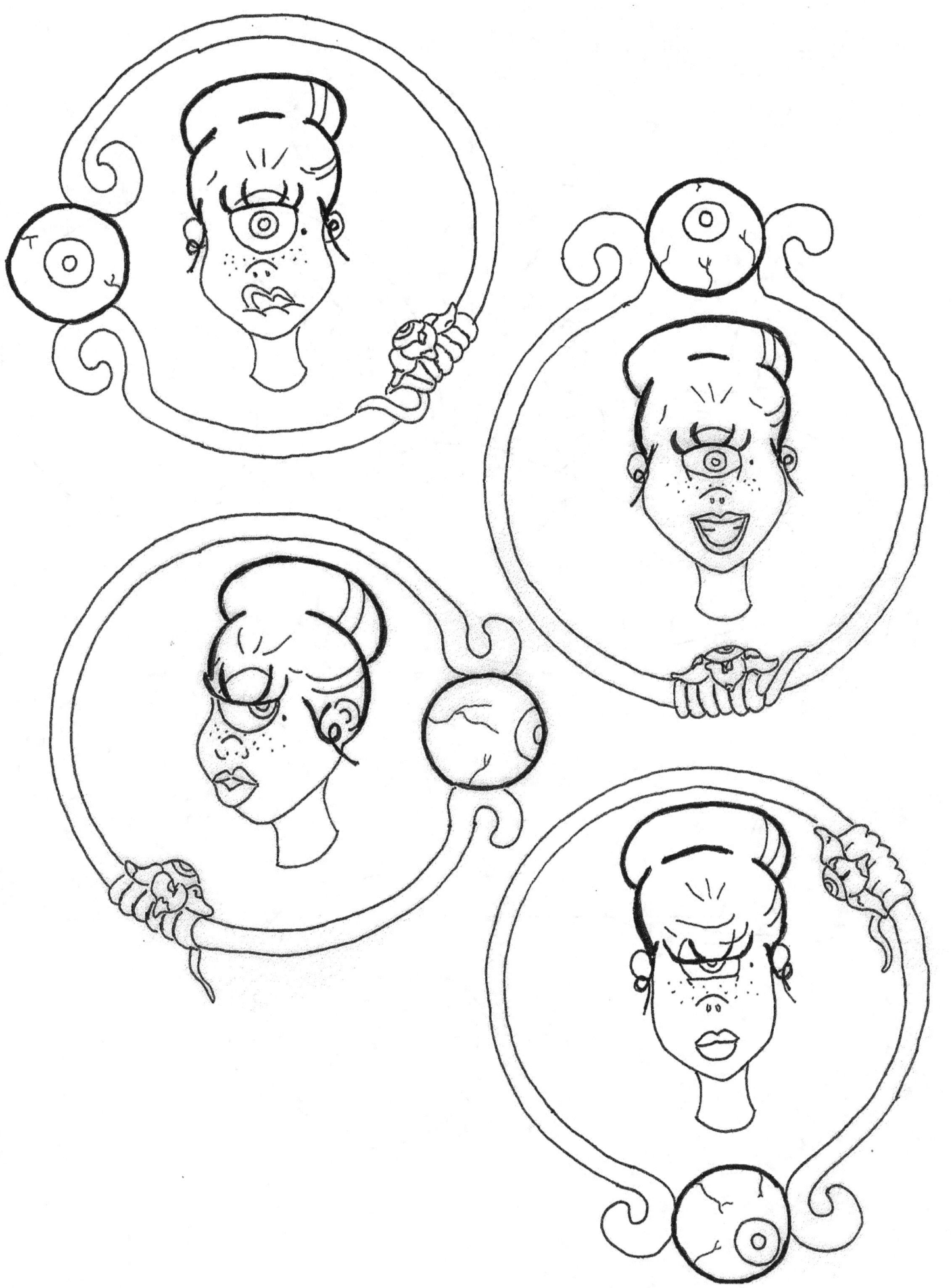

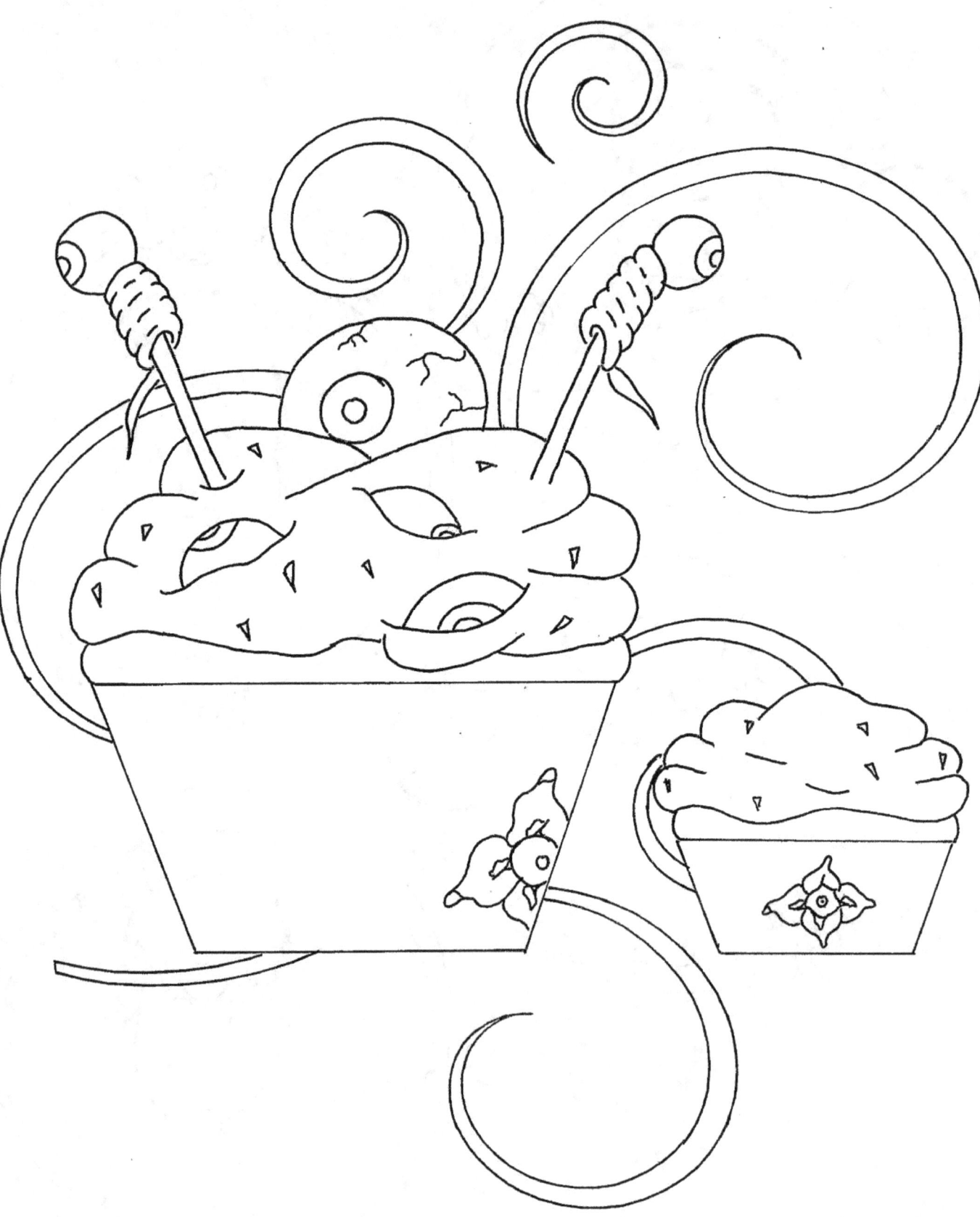

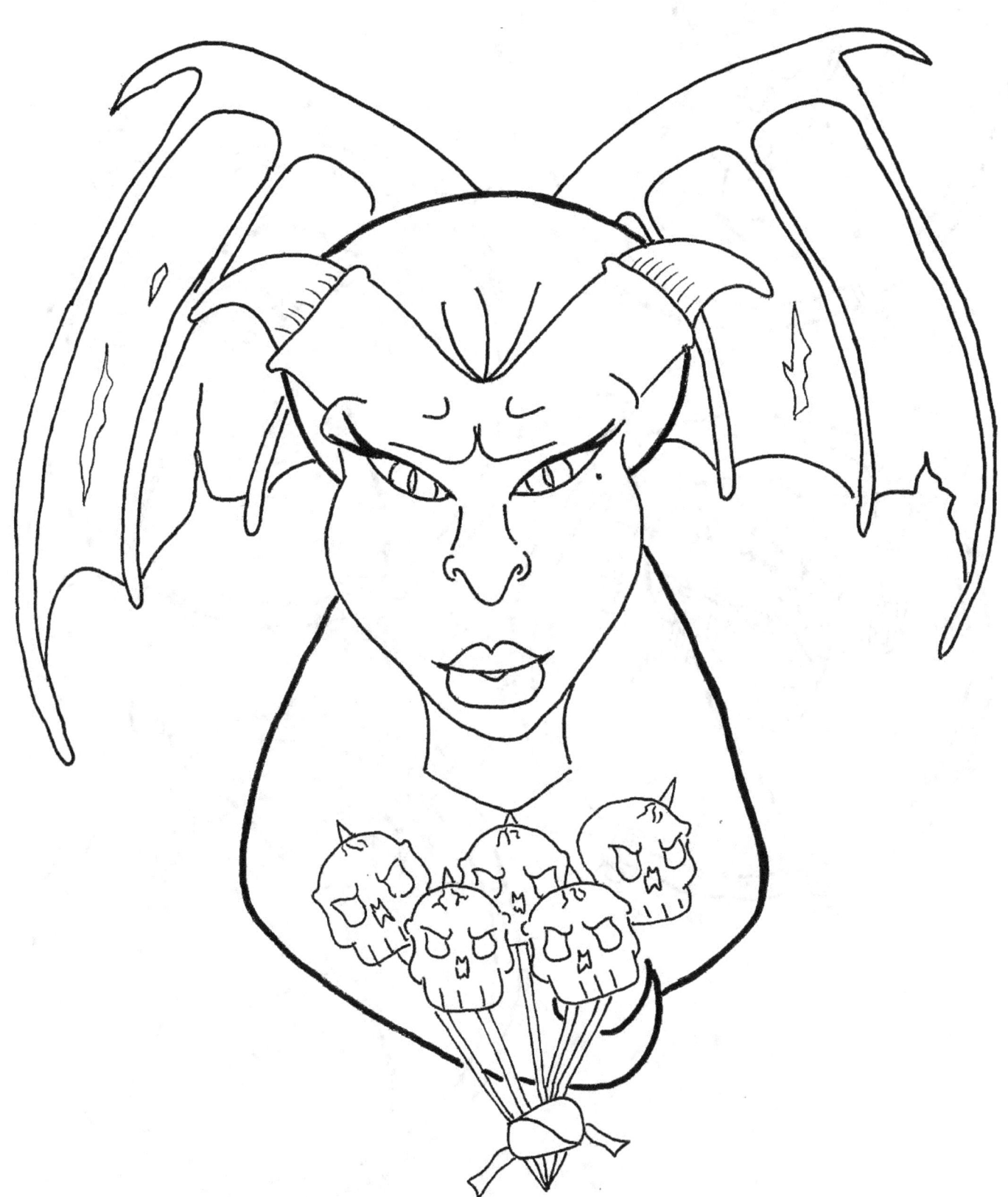

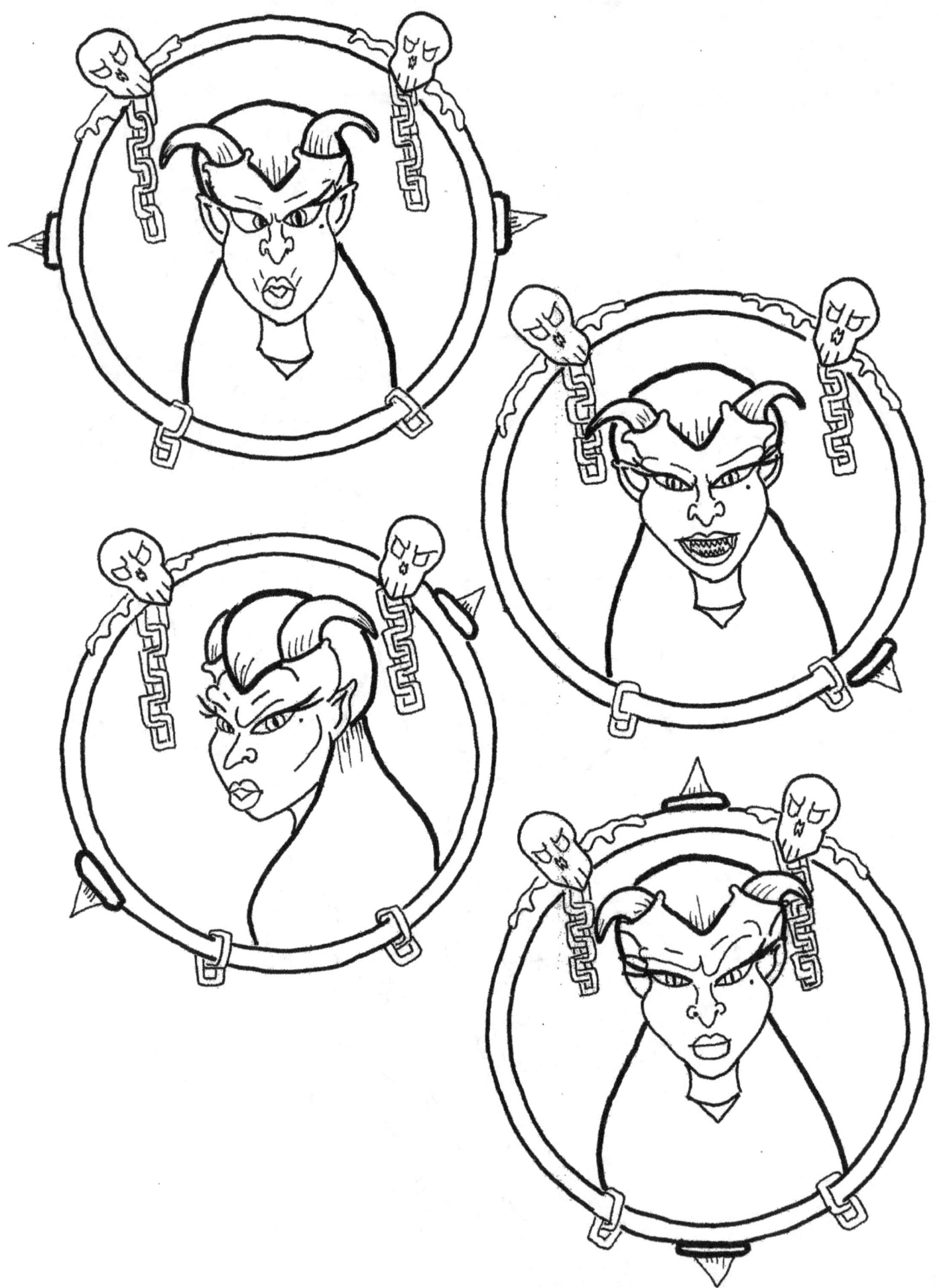

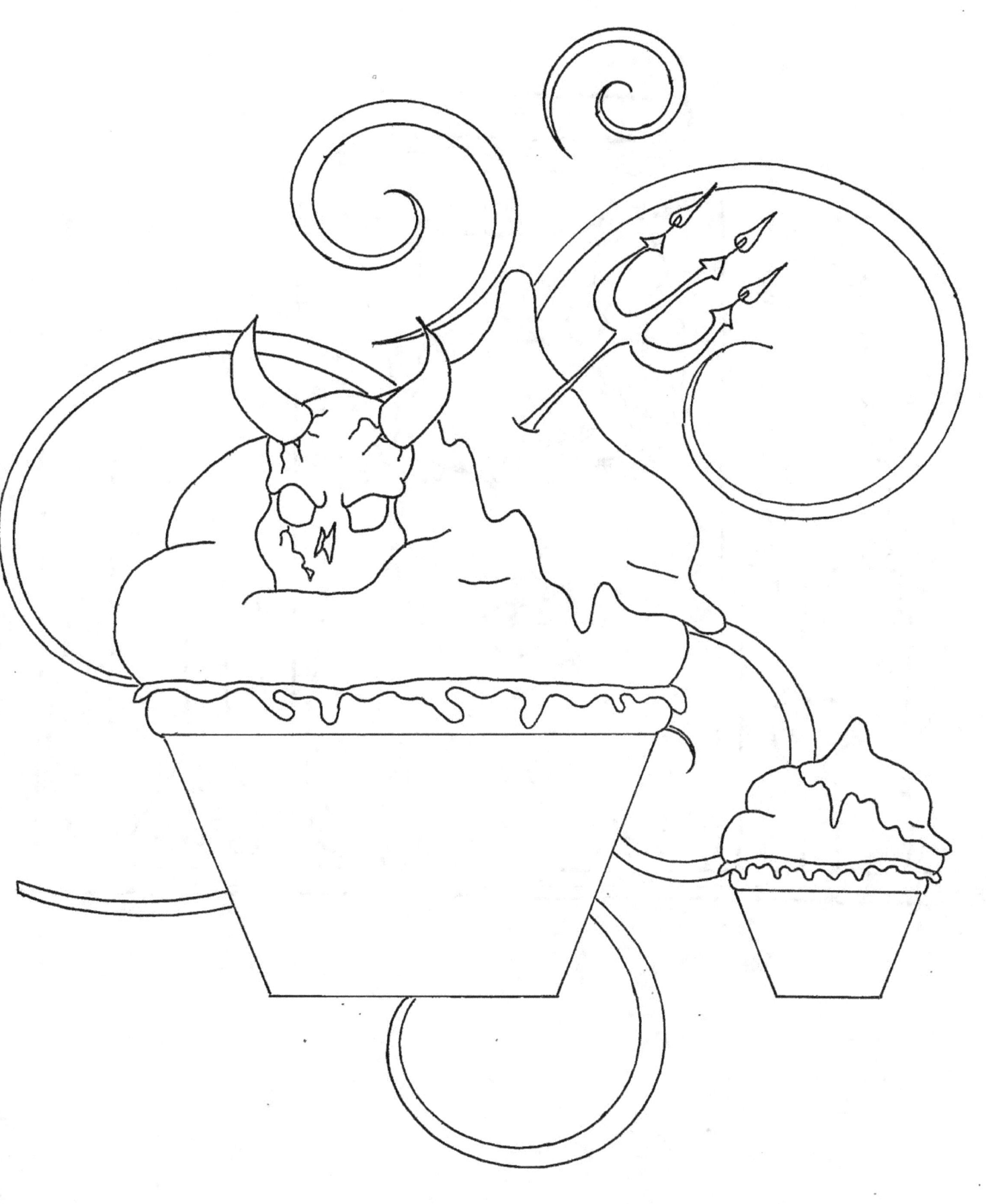

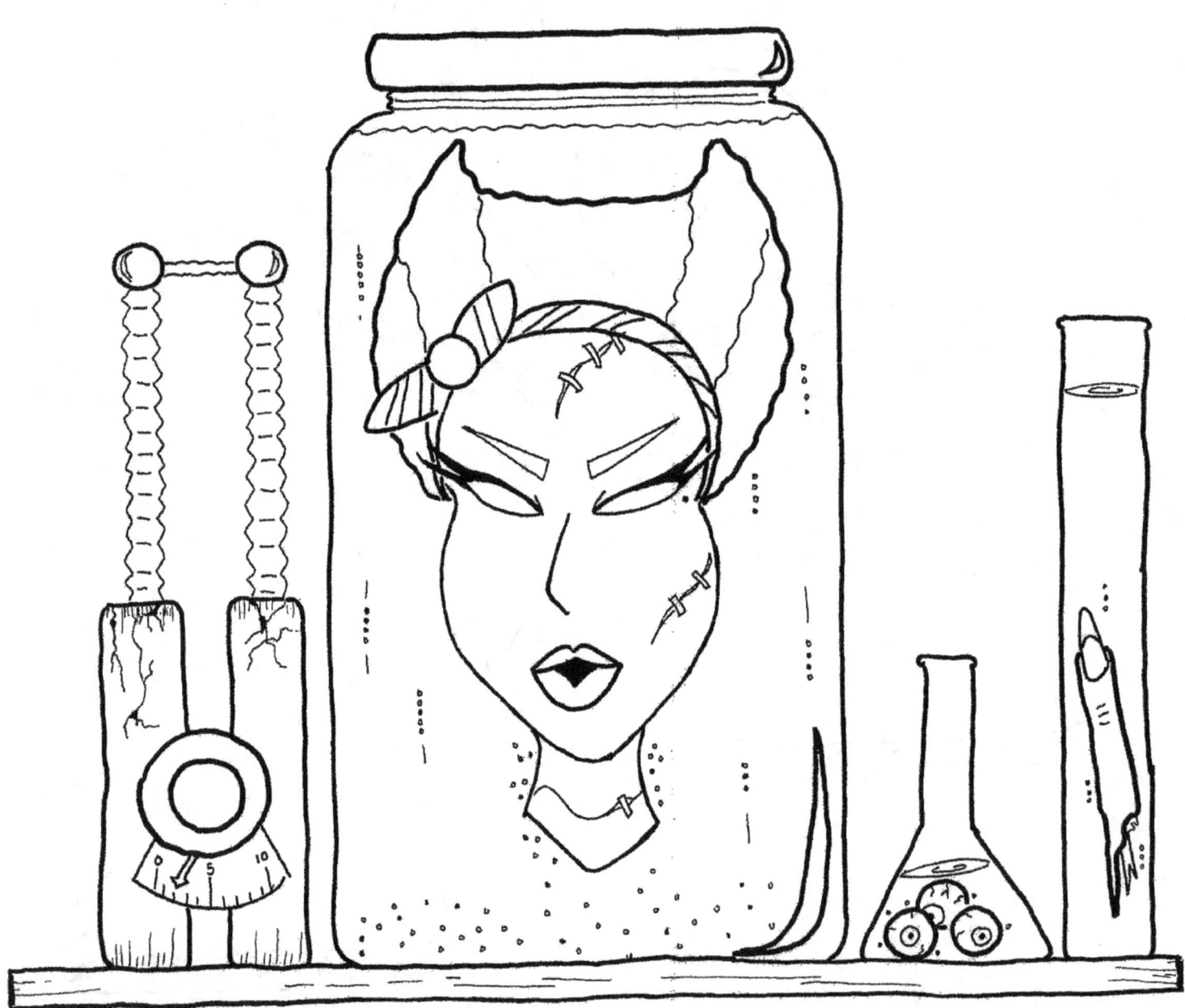

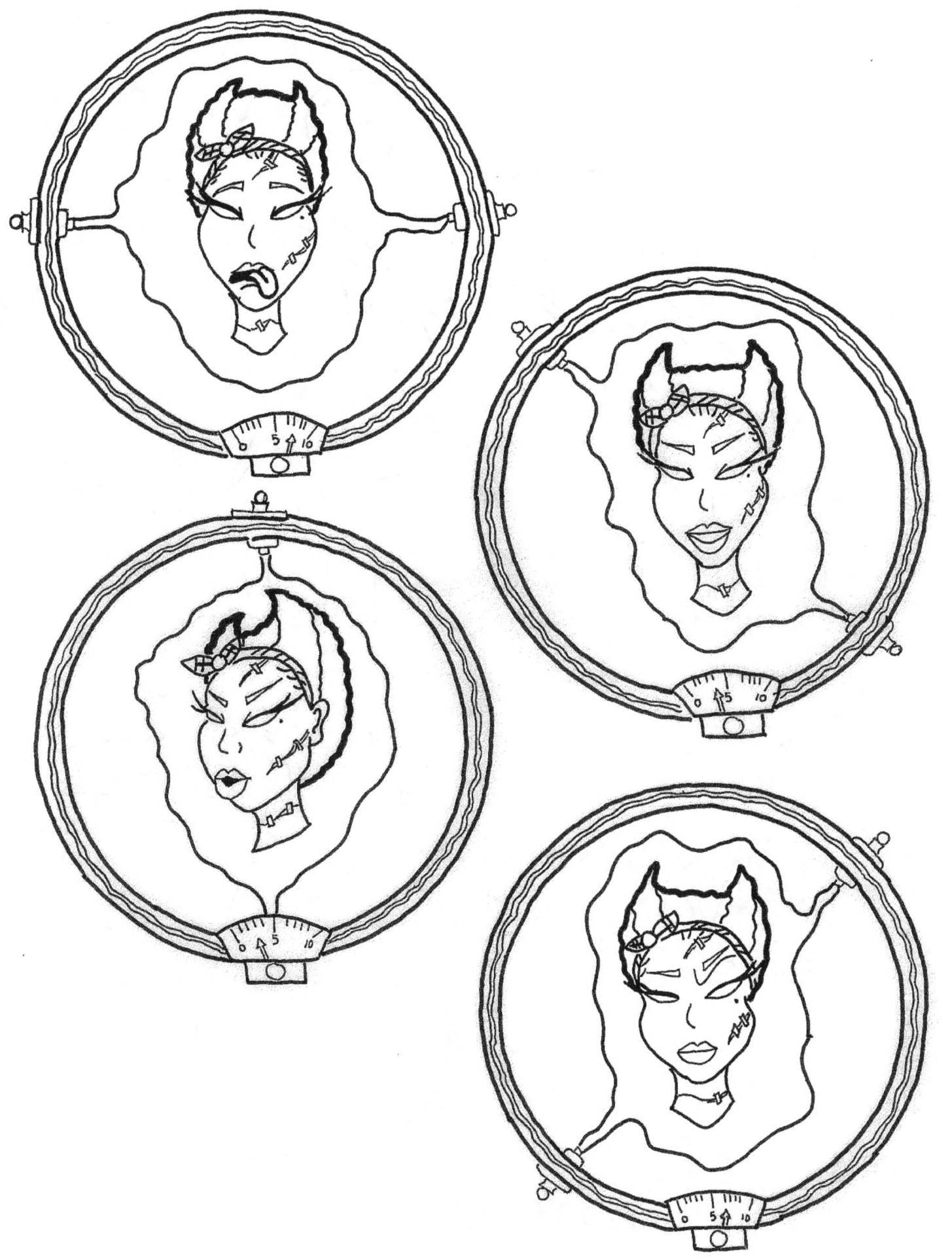

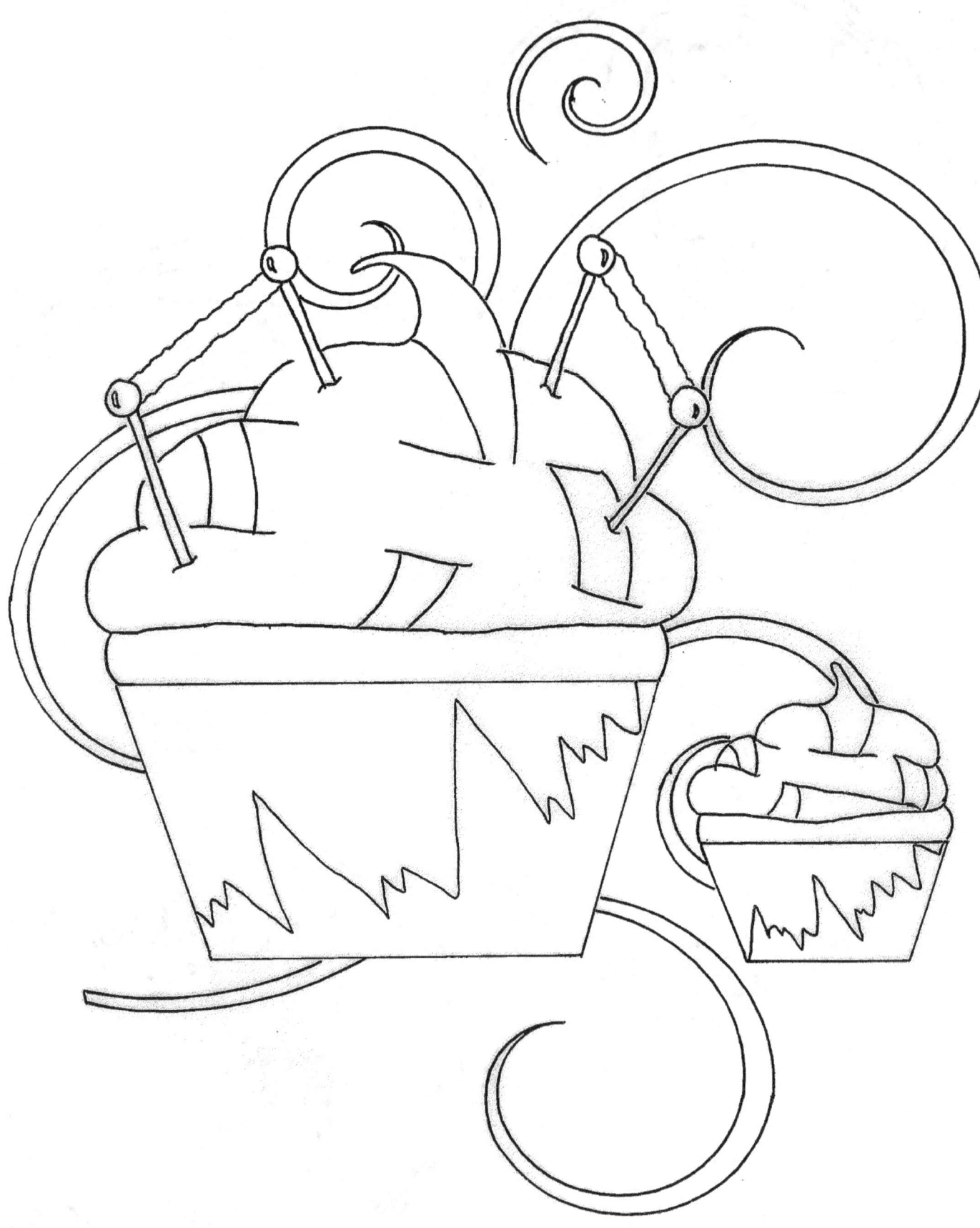

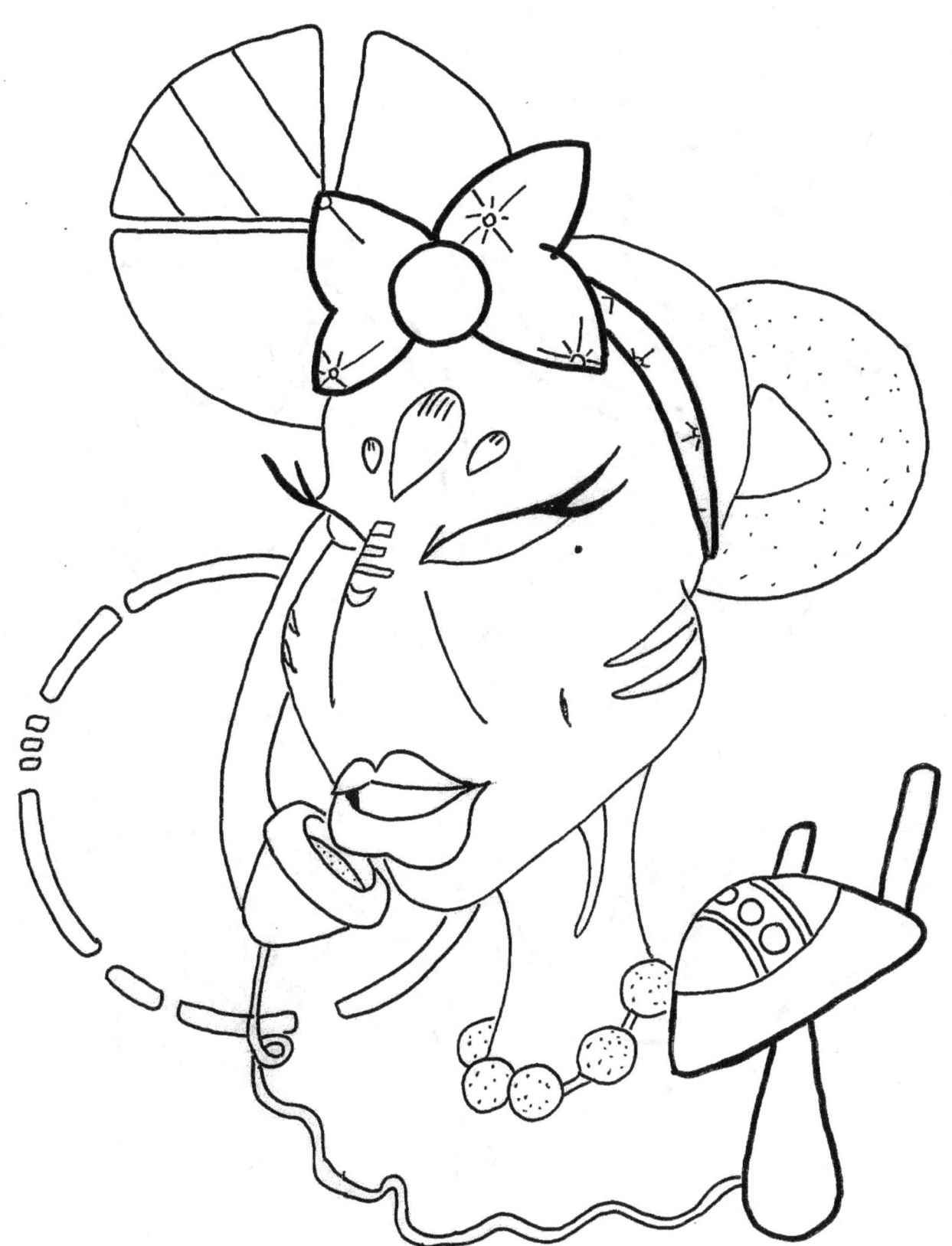

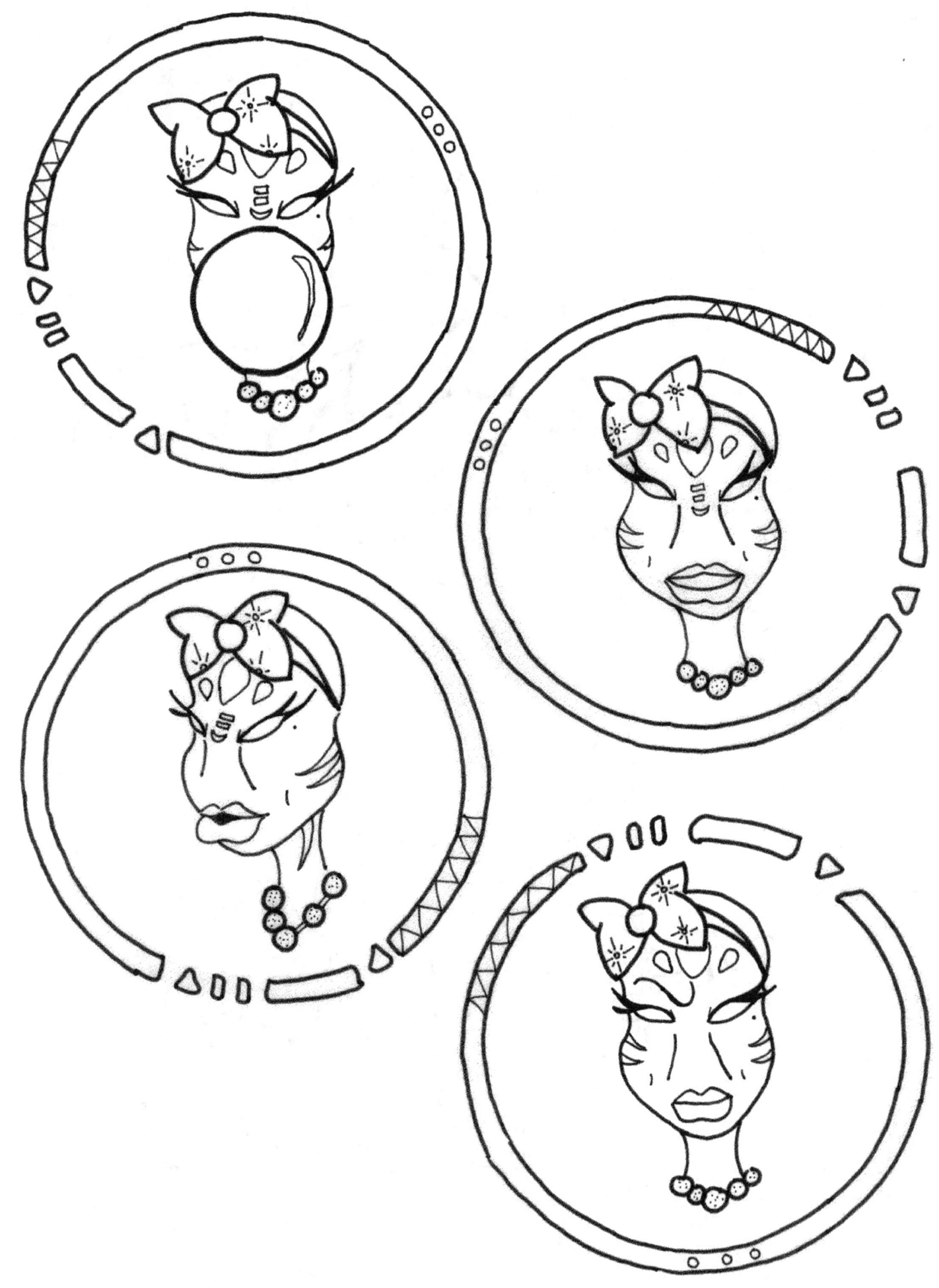

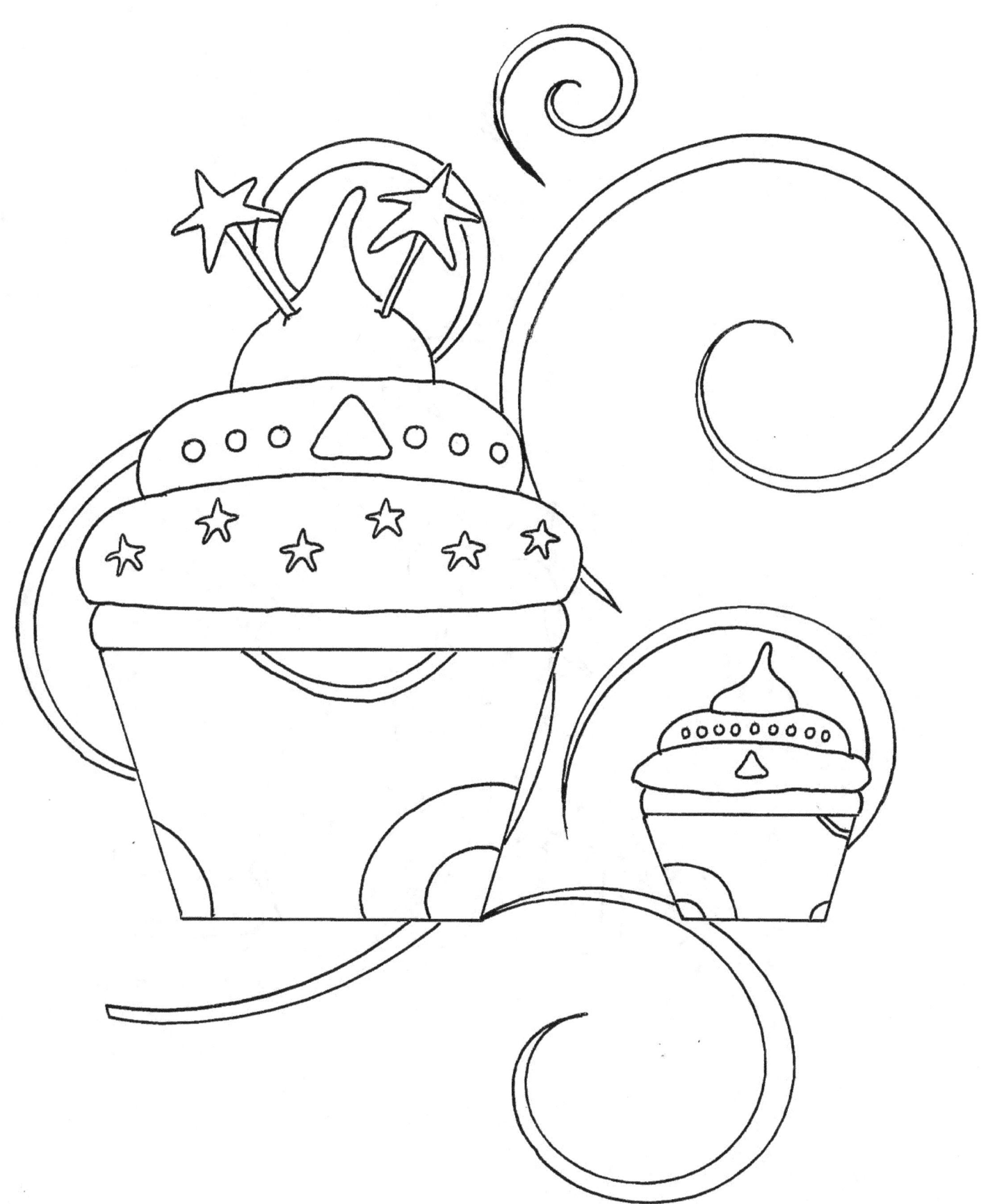

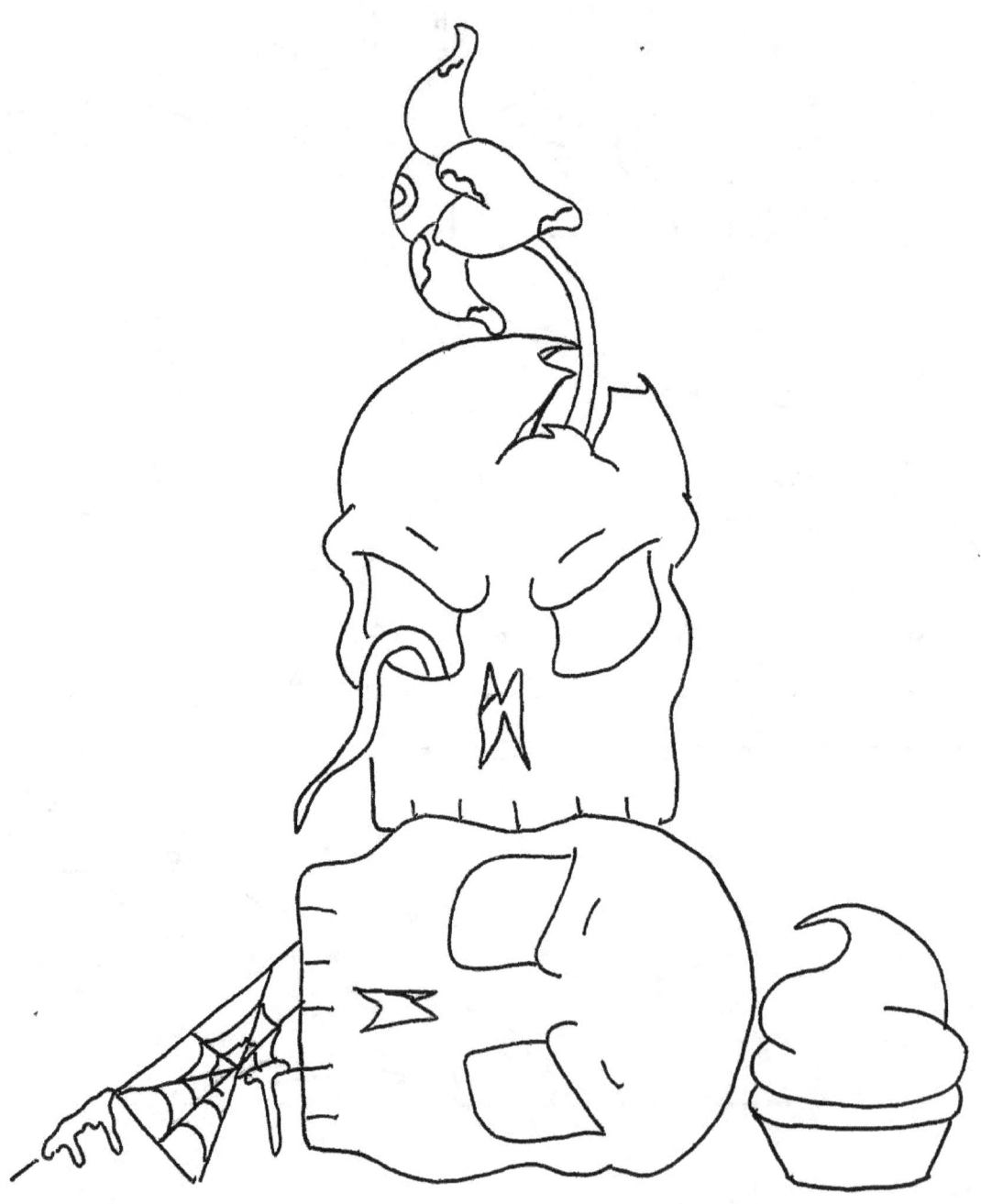

Hope you enjoyed coloring in these pages.
You can always leave me feed back or follow
me on social media. Again, Thank you for your
support

`Mz Chris

TWITTER: mzchris_art

FACEBOOK: Mz Chris Art

INSTAGRAM: mzchris_art
                   mzchriscreatez

EMAIL: mzchriscreatez@yahoo.com

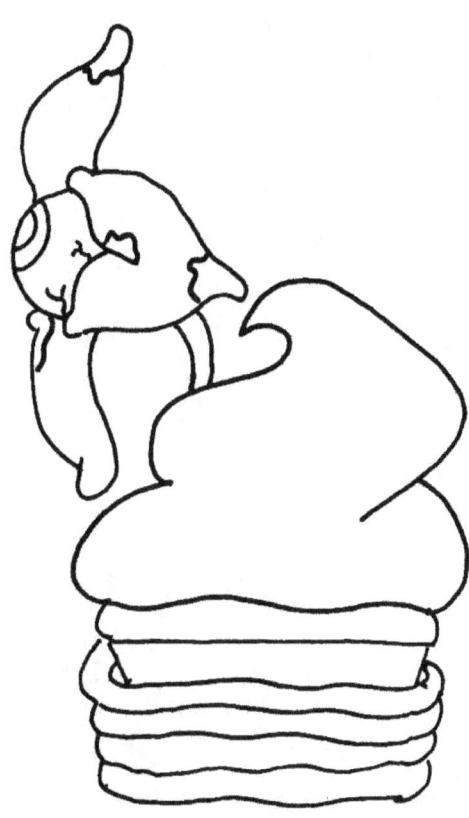

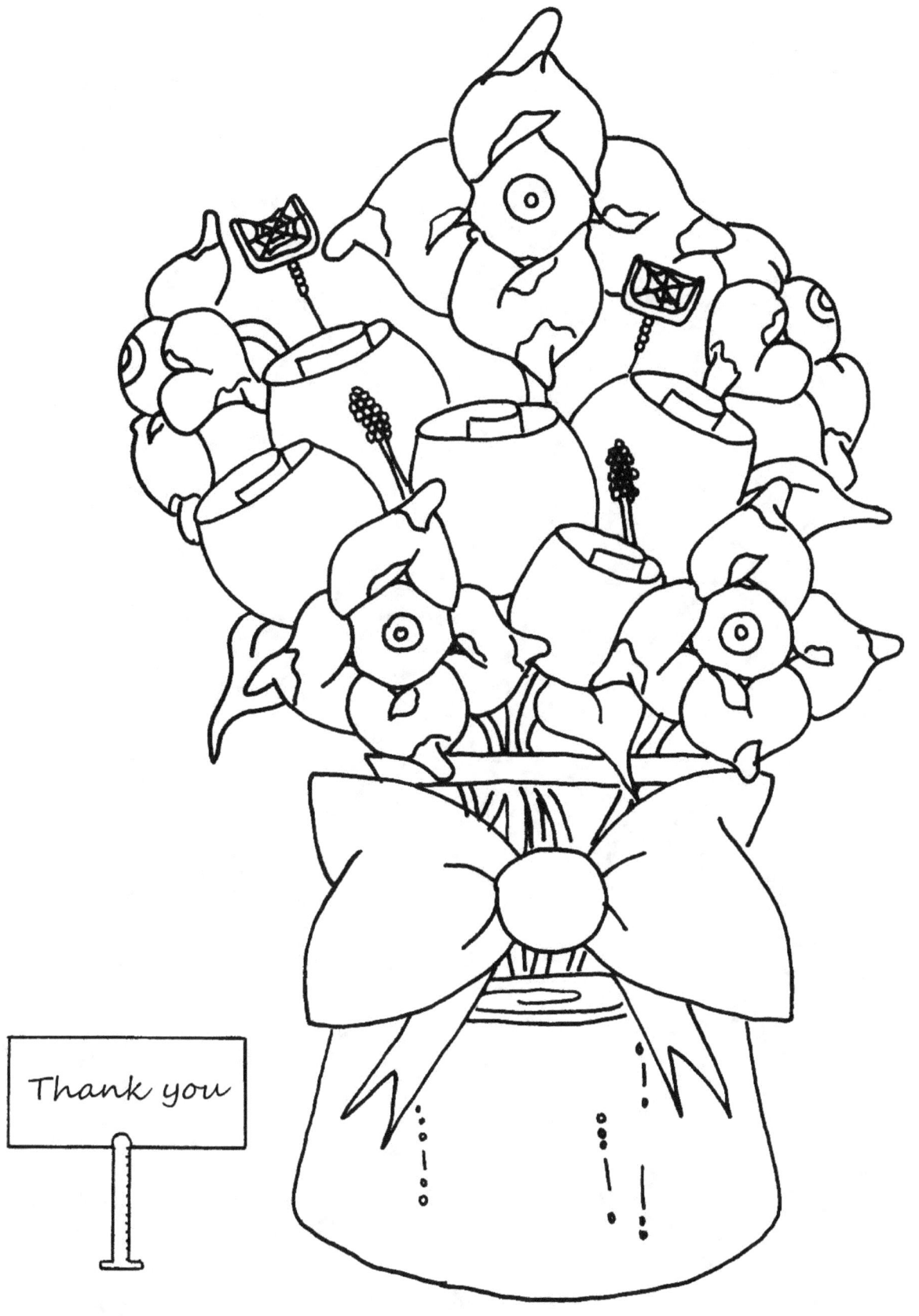

Thank you